This Fishing Journal Belongs To:

Date:
Location:  SunriseLace
Today I Went Fishing With:
my Frend

The Lure I Used Was: Wrms

Weather  Temp 45

My Catch Of The Day Was:

Fishing Trip Scale Of Awesome

⭐⭐⭐☆☆

My Fishing Notes:

Date: _____

Fishing Discoveries: _____

Date:

Location:

Today I Went Fishing With:

_____

The Lure I Used Was:

_____

Weather 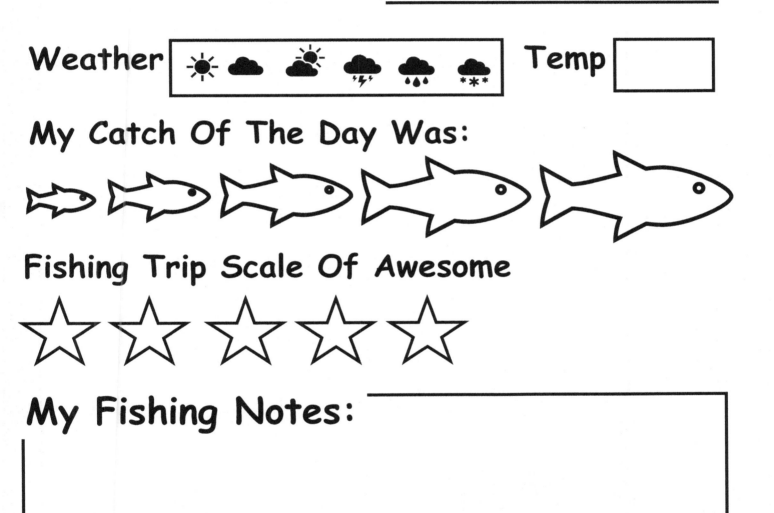 Temp

My Catch Of The Day Was:

Fishing Trip Scale Of Awesome
☆ ☆ ☆ ☆ ☆

My Fishing Notes:

Date: _____

Fishing Discoveries: _____

Date:

Location:

Today I Went Fishing With:

_____

The Lure I Used Was:

_____

Weather 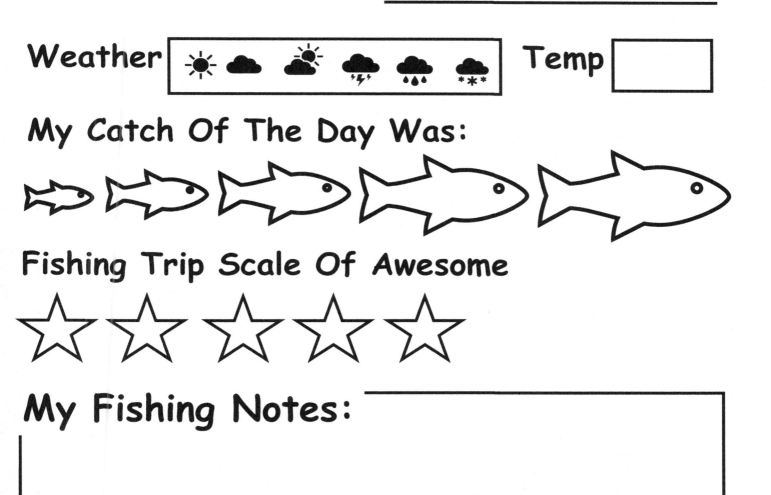 Temp

My Catch Of The Day Was:

Fishing Trip Scale Of Awesome

☆ ☆ ☆ ☆ ☆

My Fishing Notes:

Date: _____

Fishing Discoveries: _____

Date:
Location:
Today I Went Fishing With:

_____

The Lure I Used Was:

_____

Weather 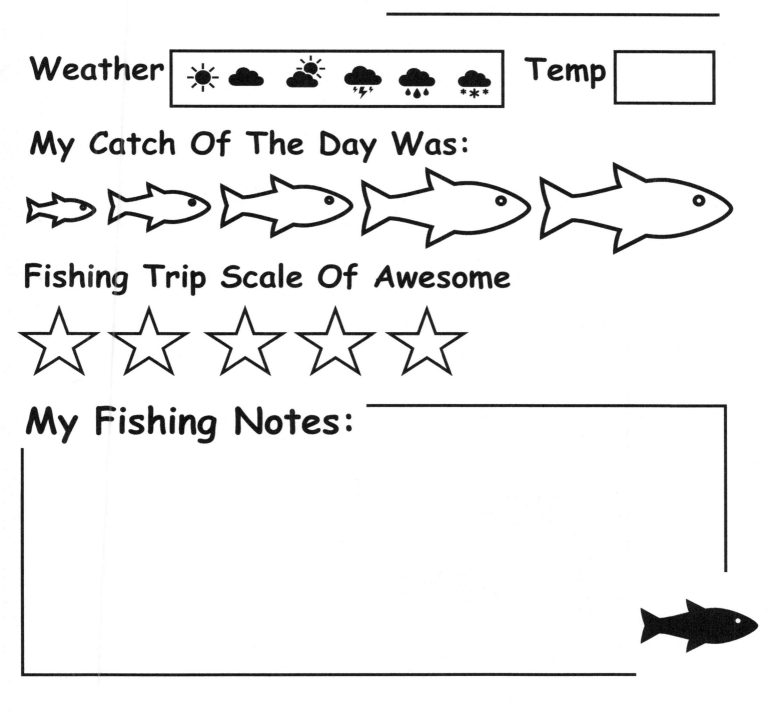 Temp

My Catch Of The Day Was:

Fishing Trip Scale Of Awesome

My Fishing Notes:

Date: _____

Fishing Discoveries: _____

Date:
Location:
Today I Went Fishing With:

_____

The Lure I Used Was:

_____

Weather 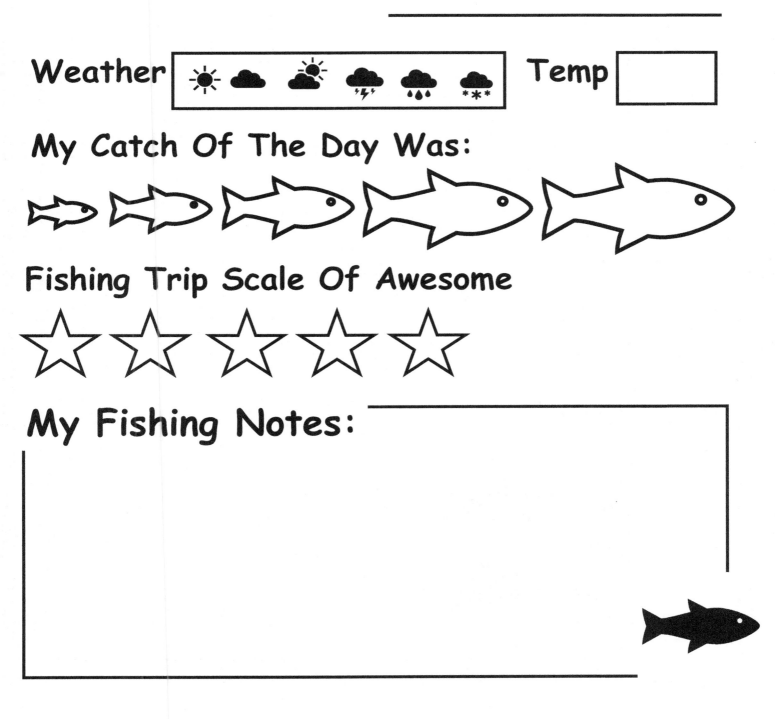 Temp

My Catch Of The Day Was:

Fishing Trip Scale Of Awesome

My Fishing Notes:

Date: _____

Fishing Discoveries: _____

Date:
Location:
Today I Went Fishing With:

_____

The Lure I Used Was:

_____

Weather 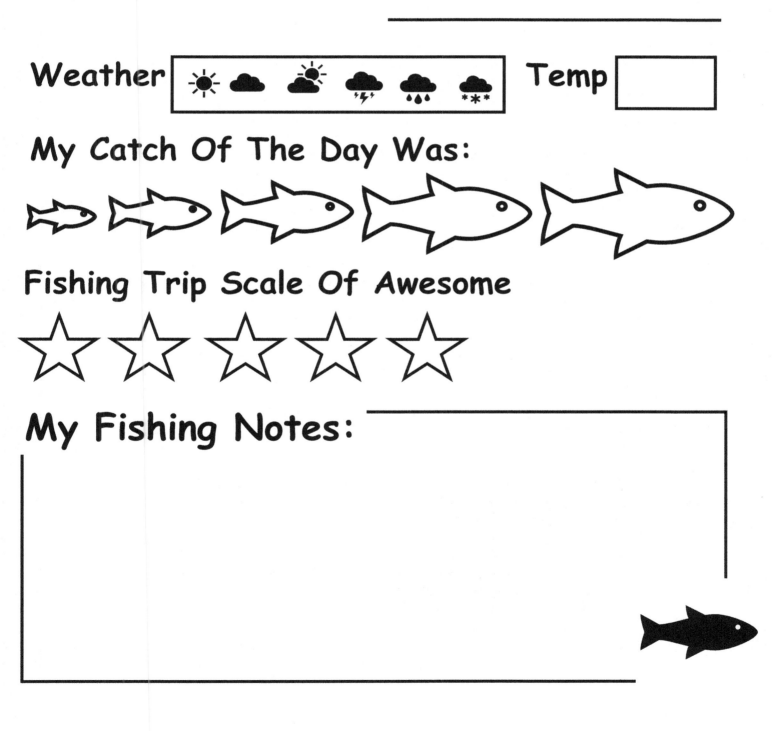 Temp

My Catch Of The Day Was:

Fishing Trip Scale Of Awesome

My Fishing Notes:

Date: _____

Fishing Discoveries: _____

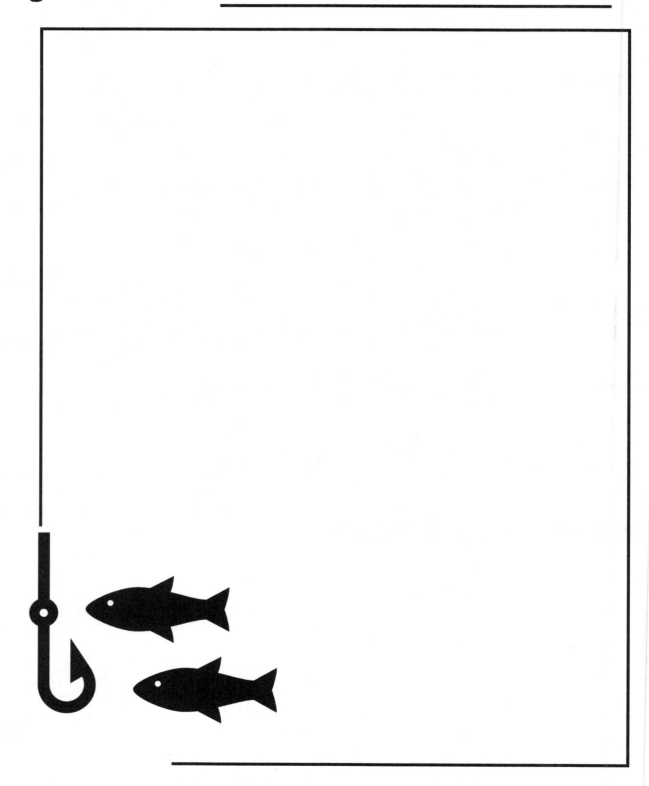

Date:
Location:
Today I Went Fishing With:

_____

The Lure I Used Was:

_____

Weather 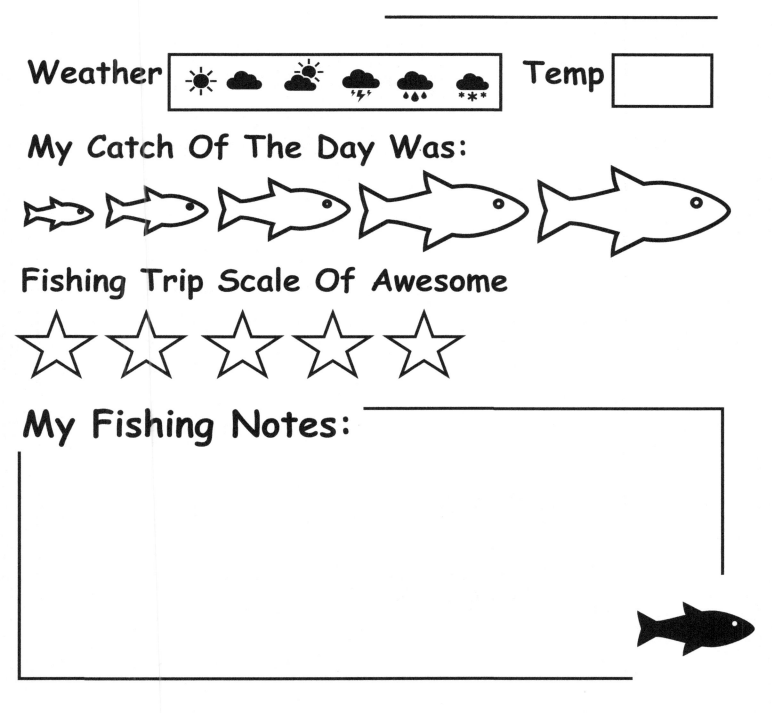 Temp

My Catch Of The Day Was:

Fishing Trip Scale Of Awesome

My Fishing Notes:

Date: _____

Fishing Discoveries: _____

Date:
Location:
Today I Went Fishing With:

_____

The Lure I Used Was:

_____

Weather 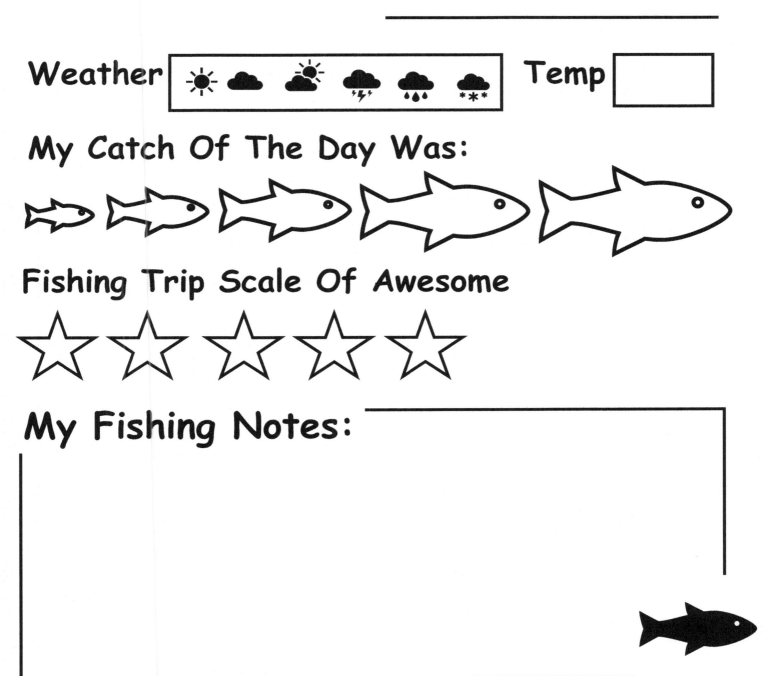 Temp

My Catch Of The Day Was:

Fishing Trip Scale Of Awesome

My Fishing Notes:

Date: _____

Fishing Discoveries: _____

Date:

Location:

Today I Went Fishing With:

_____

The Lure I Used Was:

_____

Weather 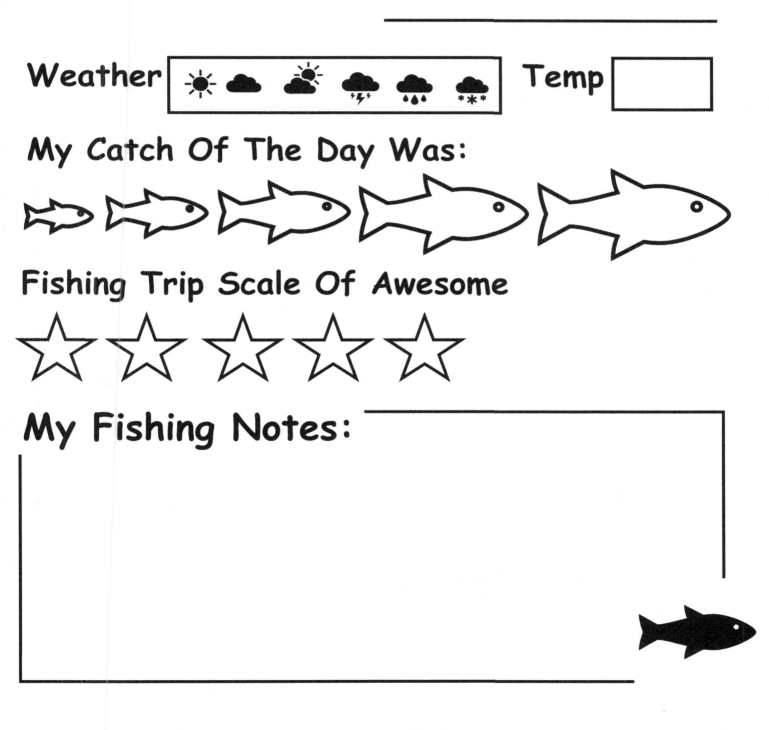 Temp

My Catch Of The Day Was:

Fishing Trip Scale Of Awesome

My Fishing Notes:

Date: _____

Fishing Discoveries: _____

Date:
Location:
Today I Went Fishing With:

_____

The Lure I Used Was:

_____

Weather 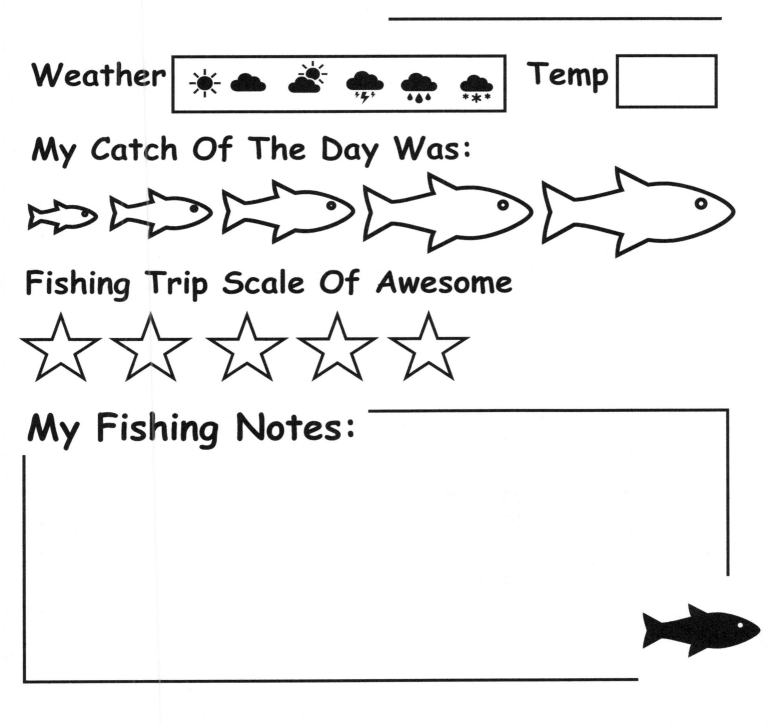 Temp

My Catch Of The Day Was:

Fishing Trip Scale Of Awesome

My Fishing Notes:

Date: _____

Fishing Discoveries: _____

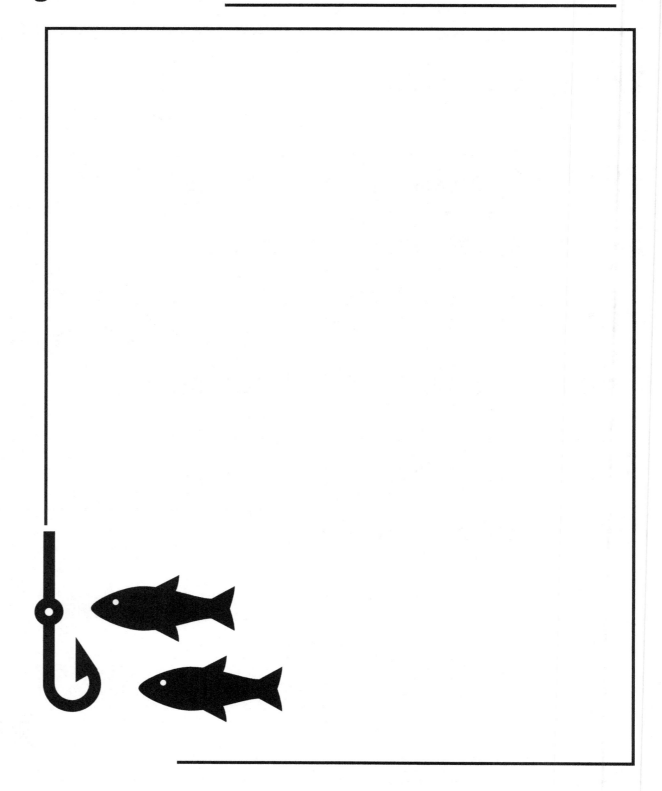

Date:

Location:

Today I Went Fishing With:

_____

The Lure I Used Was:

_____

Weather 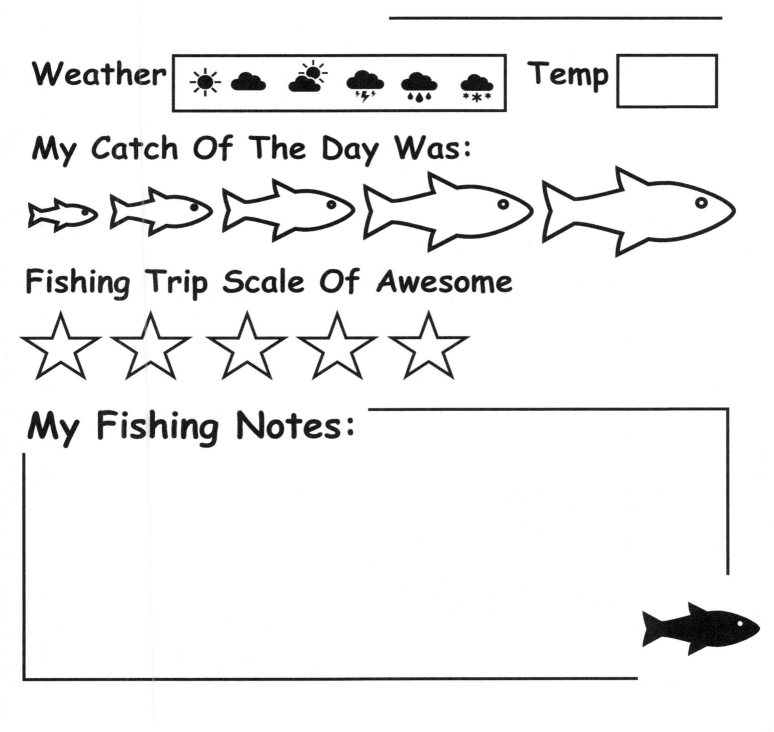 Temp

My Catch Of The Day Was:

Fishing Trip Scale Of Awesome

☆ ☆ ☆ ☆ ☆

My Fishing Notes:

Date: _____

Fishing Discoveries: _____

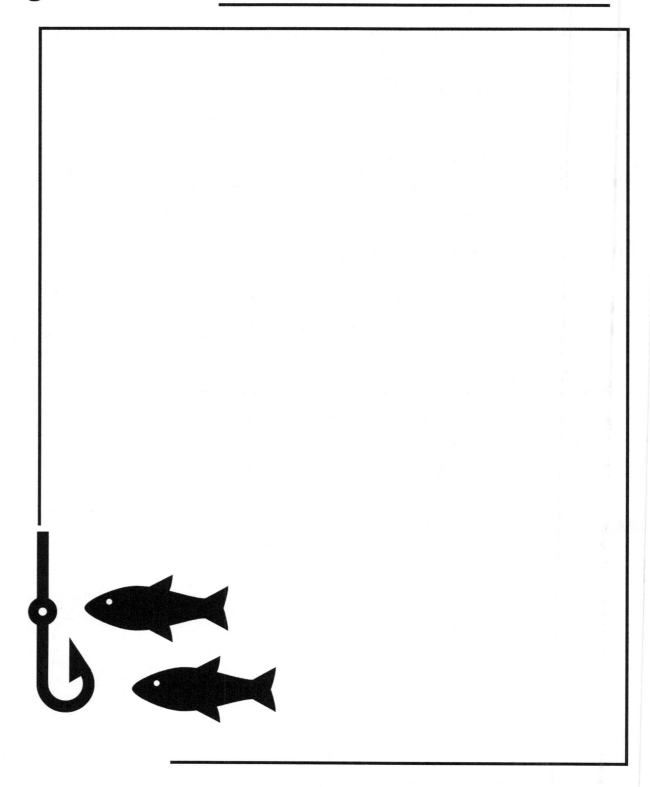

Date:
Location:
Today I Went Fishing With:

_____

The Lure I Used Was:

_____

Weather 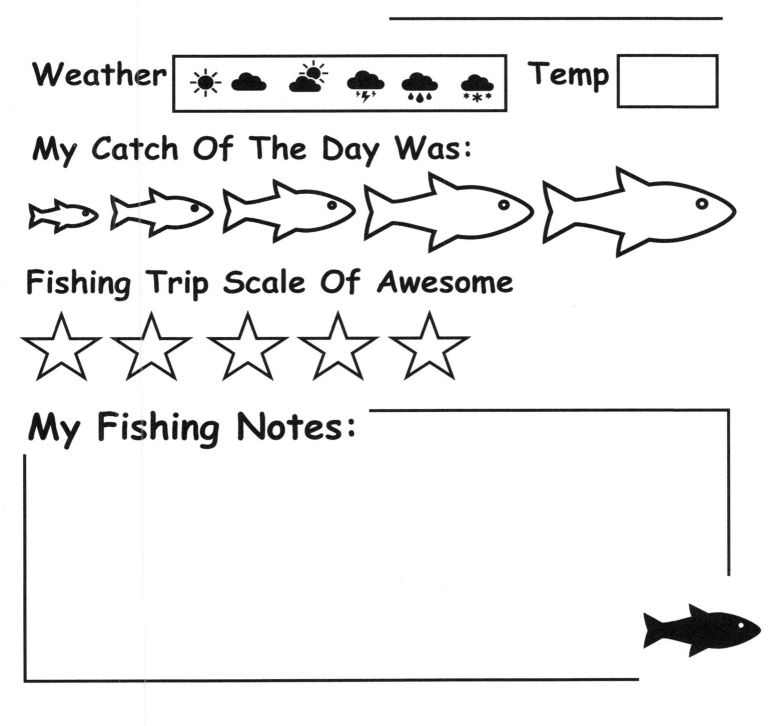 Temp

My Catch Of The Day Was:

Fishing Trip Scale Of Awesome

My Fishing Notes:

Date: _____

Fishing Discoveries: _____

Date:
Location:
Today I Went Fishing With:

_____

The Lure I Used Was:

_____

Weather 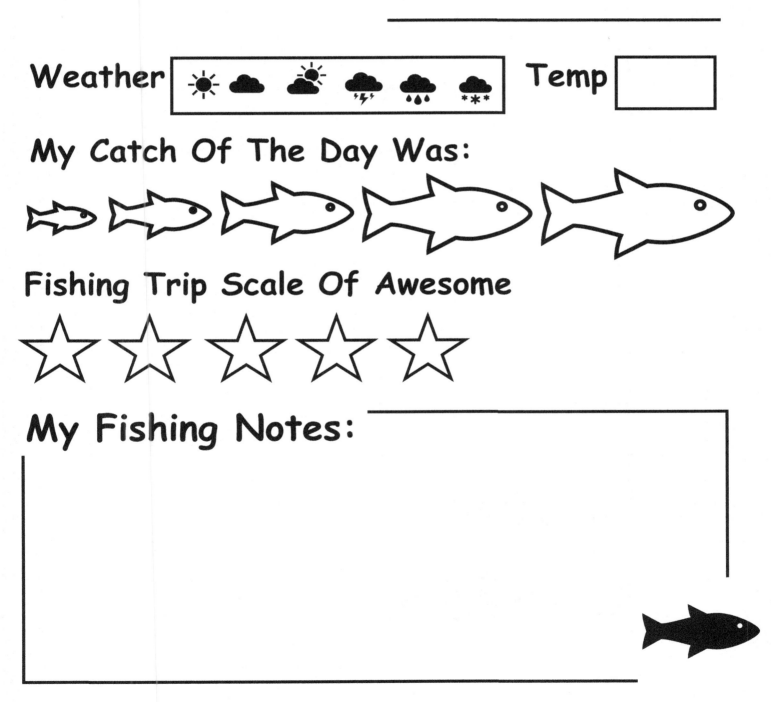 Temp

My Catch Of The Day Was:

Fishing Trip Scale Of Awesome

My Fishing Notes:

Date: _____

Fishing Discoveries: _____

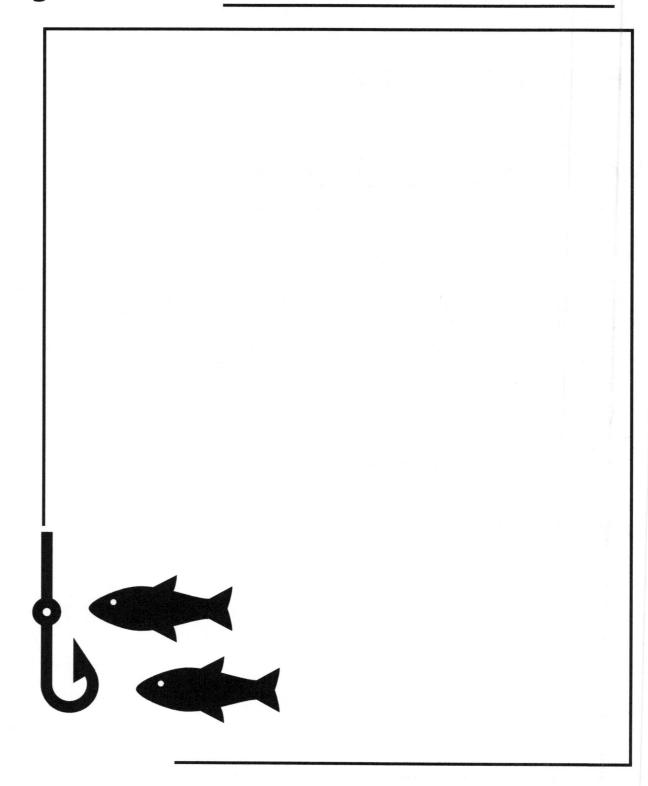

Date:

Location:

Today I Went Fishing With:

_____

The Lure I Used Was:

_____

Weather 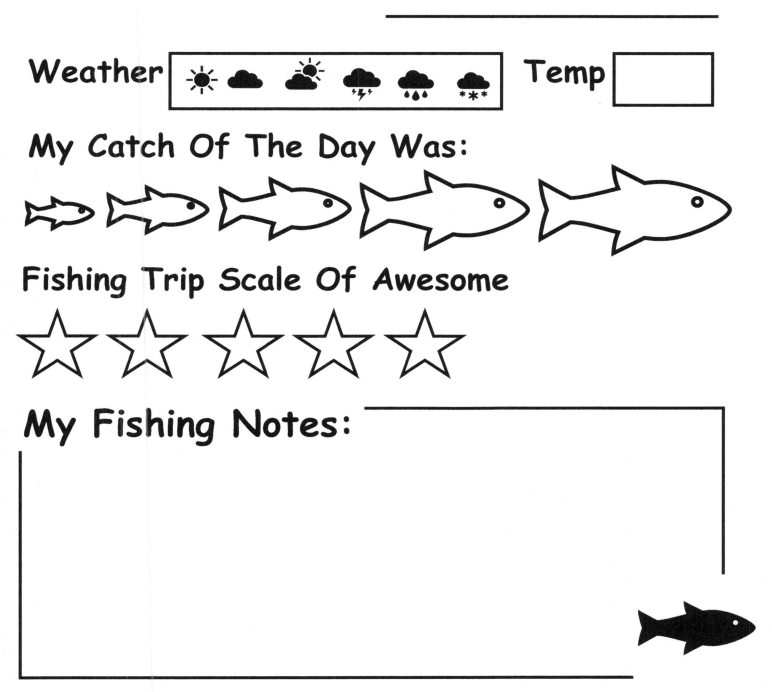 Temp

My Catch Of The Day Was:

Fishing Trip Scale Of Awesome

My Fishing Notes:

Date: _____

Fishing Discoveries: _____

Date:
Location:
Today I Went Fishing With:

_____

The Lure I Used Was:

_____

Weather 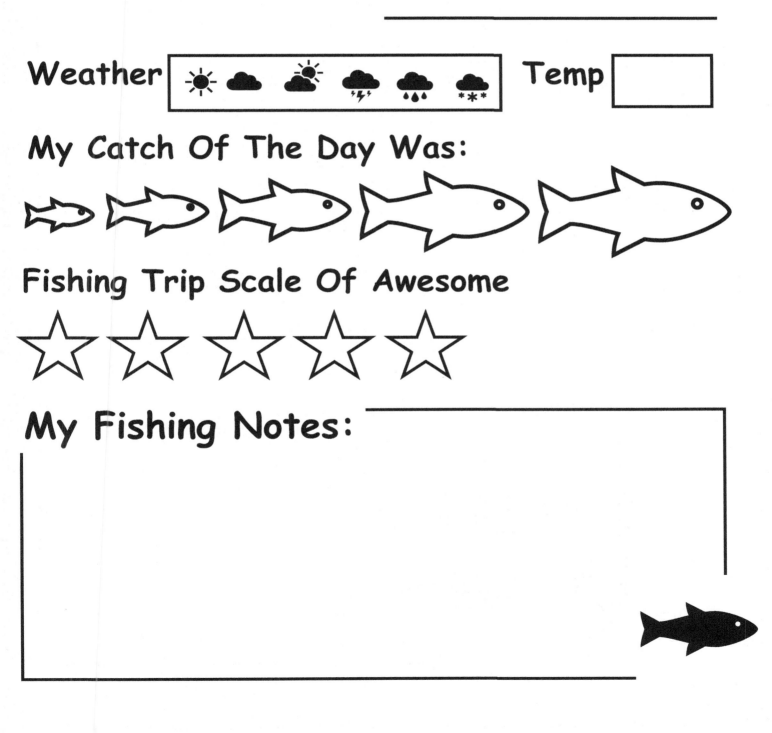 Temp

My Catch Of The Day Was:

Fishing Trip Scale Of Awesome

My Fishing Notes:

Date: _____

Fishing Discoveries: _____

Date:
Location:
Today I Went Fishing With:

_____

The Lure I Used Was:

_____

Weather 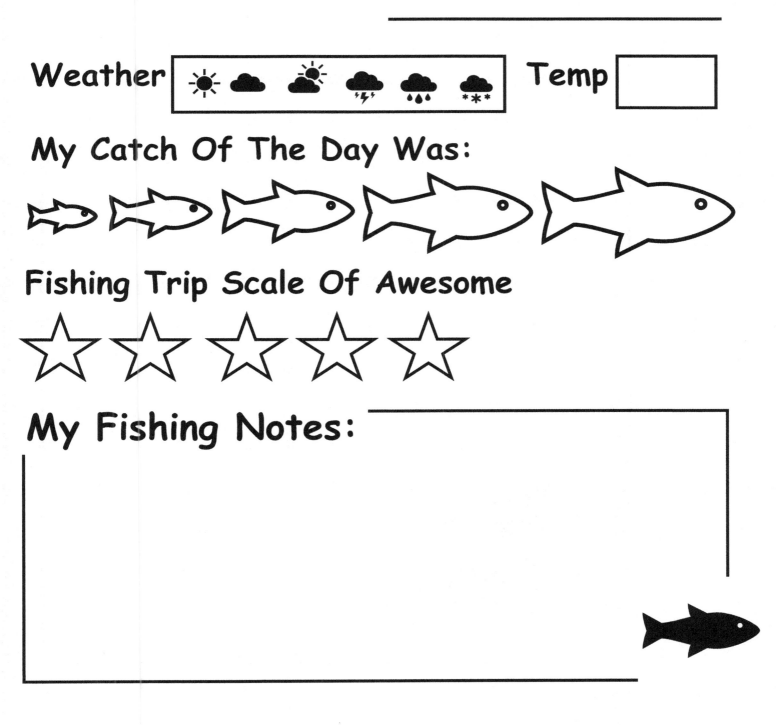 Temp

My Catch Of The Day Was:

Fishing Trip Scale Of Awesome

My Fishing Notes:

Date: _____

Fishing Discoveries: _____

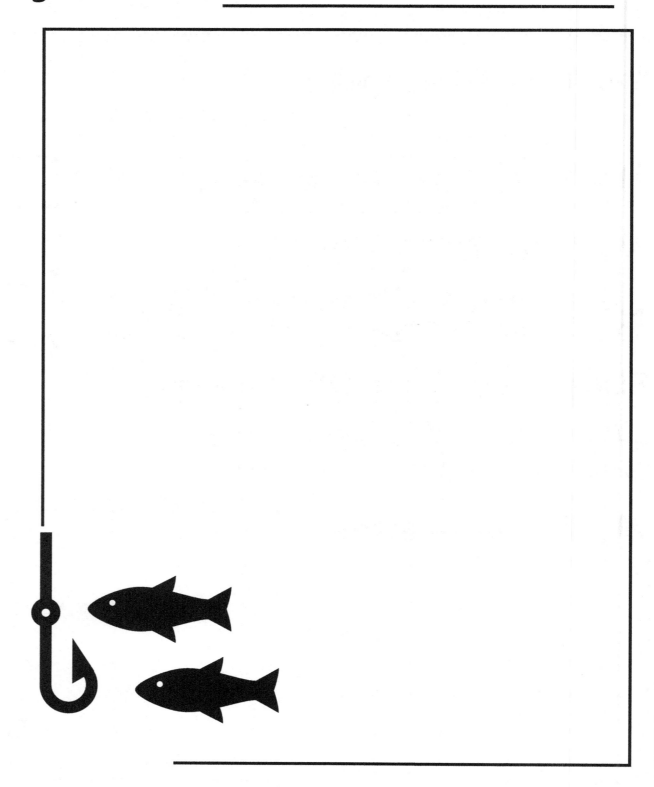

Date:

Location:

Today I Went Fishing With:

_____

The Lure I Used Was:

Weather 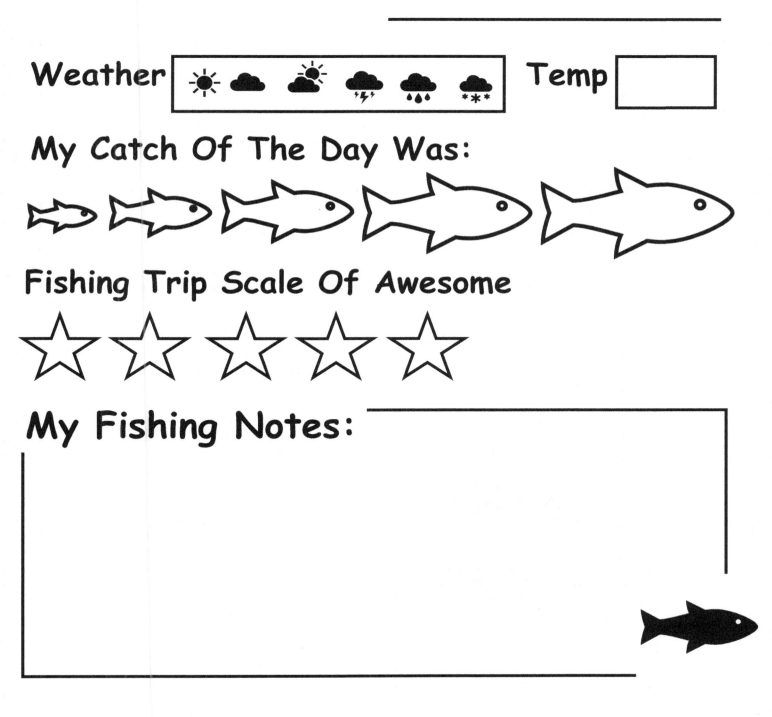 Temp

My Catch Of The Day Was:

Fishing Trip Scale Of Awesome

My Fishing Notes:

Date: _____

Fishing Discoveries: _____

Date:
Location:
Today I Went Fishing With:

_____

The Lure I Used Was:

_____

Weather 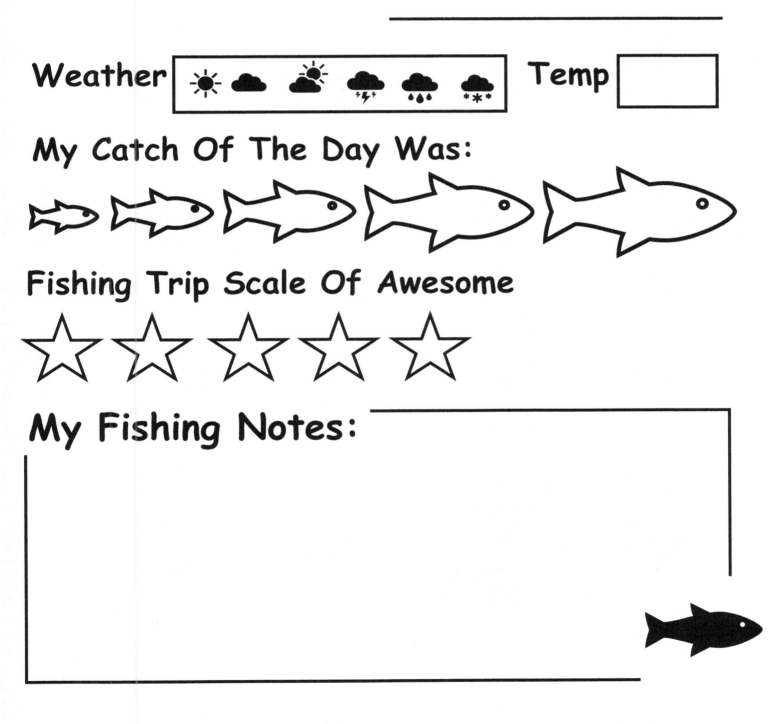 Temp

My Catch Of The Day Was:

Fishing Trip Scale Of Awesome

My Fishing Notes:

Date: _____

Fishing Discoveries: _____

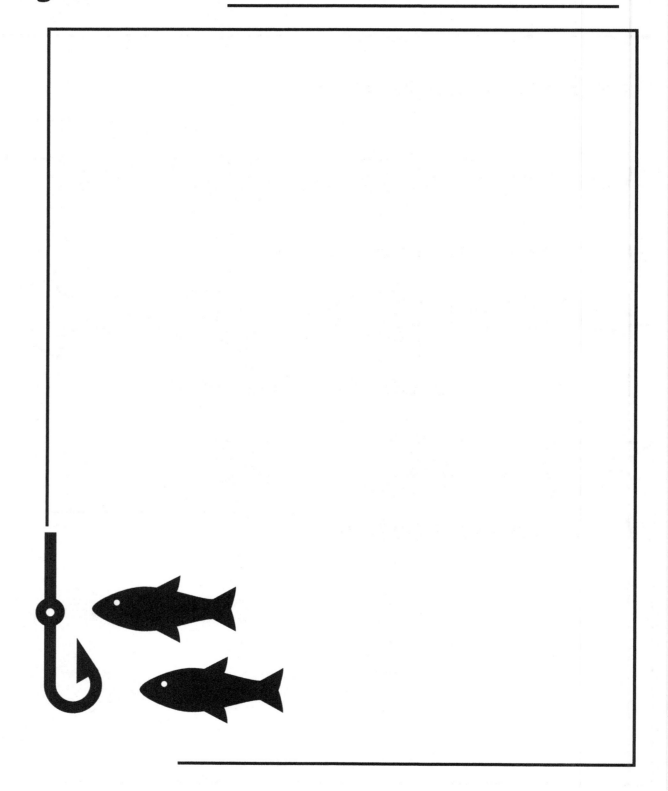

Date:

Location:

Today I Went Fishing With:

_____

The Lure I Used Was:

_____

Weather 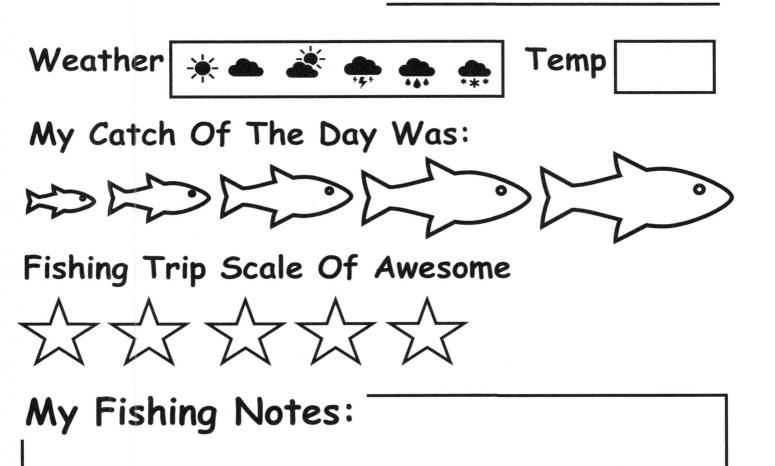 Temp

My Catch Of The Day Was:

Fishing Trip Scale Of Awesome

☆ ☆ ☆ ☆ ☆

My Fishing Notes:

Date: _____

Fishing Discoveries: _____

Date:
Location:
Today I Went Fishing With:

_____

The Lure I Used Was:

_____

Weather 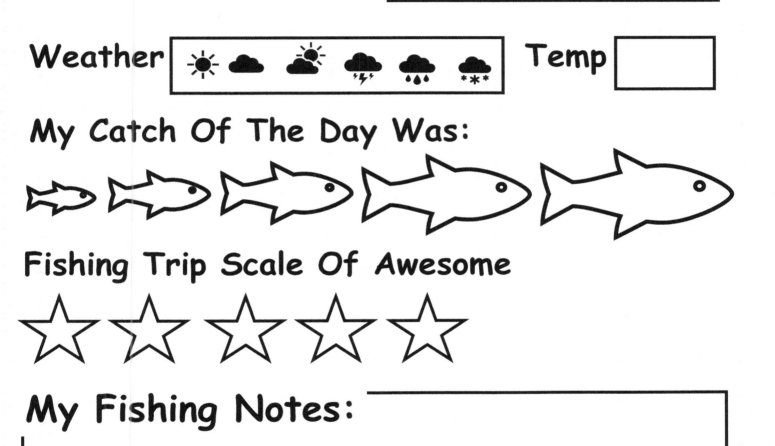 Temp

My Catch Of The Day Was:

Fishing Trip Scale Of Awesome
☆ ☆ ☆ ☆ ☆

My Fishing Notes:

Date: _____

Fishing Discoveries: _____

Date:
Location:
Today I Went Fishing With:

_____

The Lure I Used Was:

_____

Weather 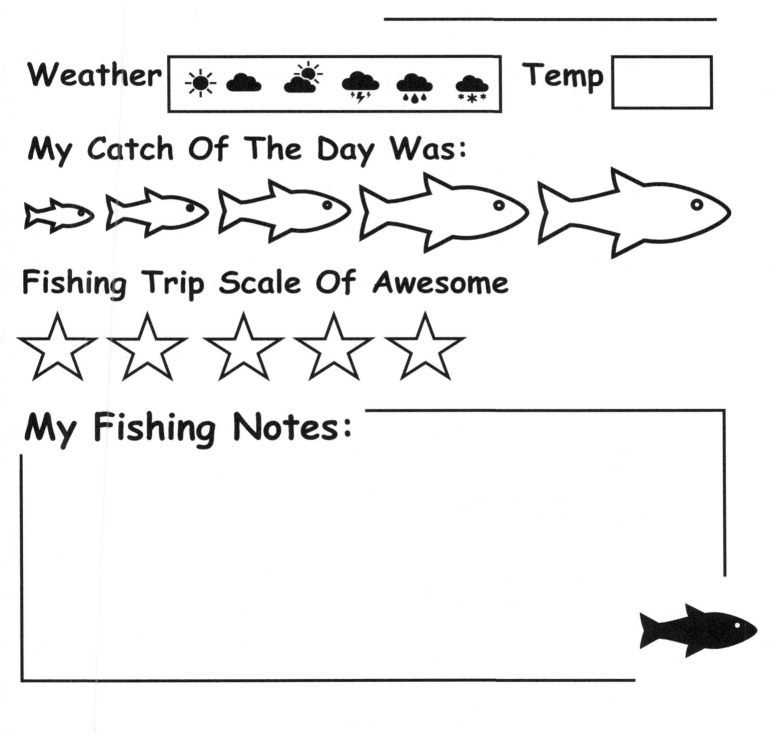 Temp

My Catch Of The Day Was:

Fishing Trip Scale Of Awesome

My Fishing Notes:

Date: _____

Fishing Discoveries: _____

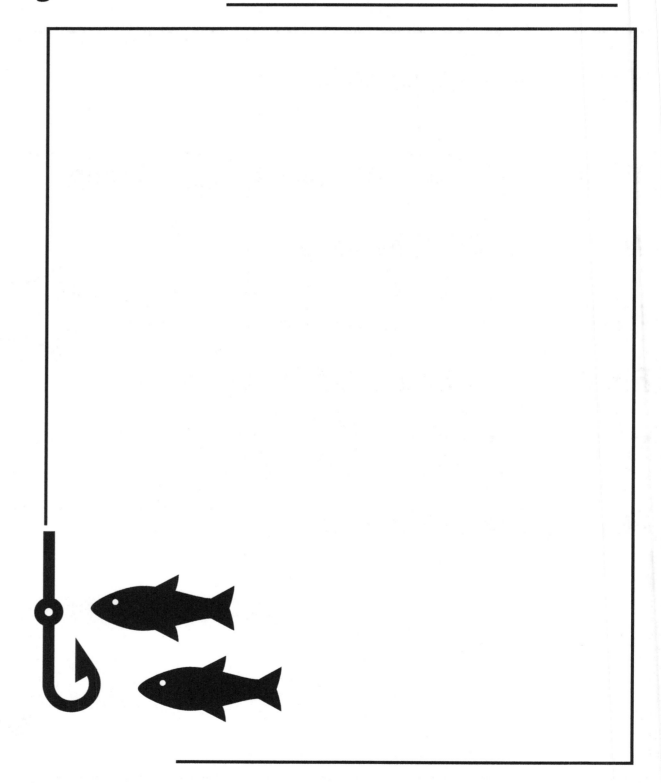

Date:

Location:

Today I Went Fishing With:

_____

The Lure I Used Was:

_____

Weather 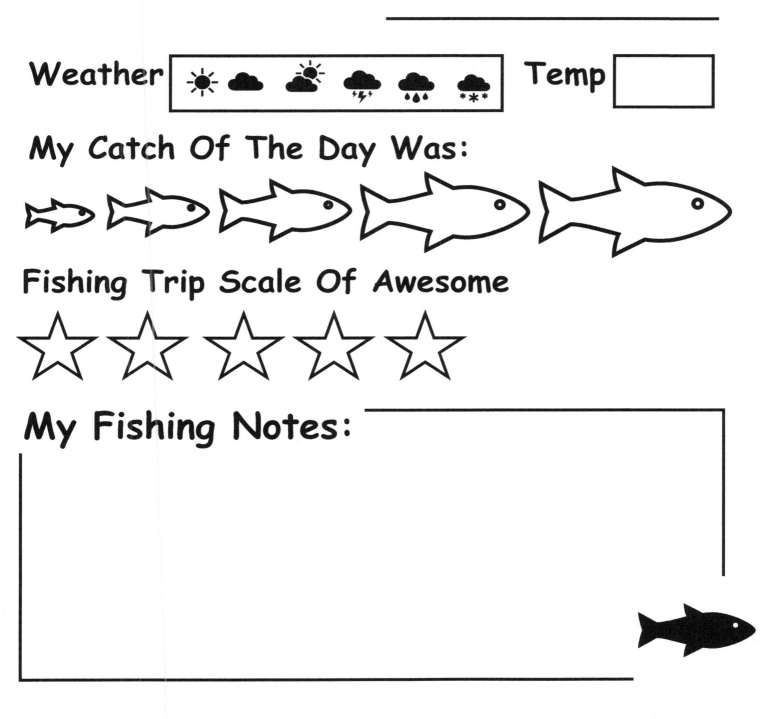 Temp

My Catch Of The Day Was:

Fishing Trip Scale Of Awesome

My Fishing Notes:

Date: _____

Fishing Discoveries: _____

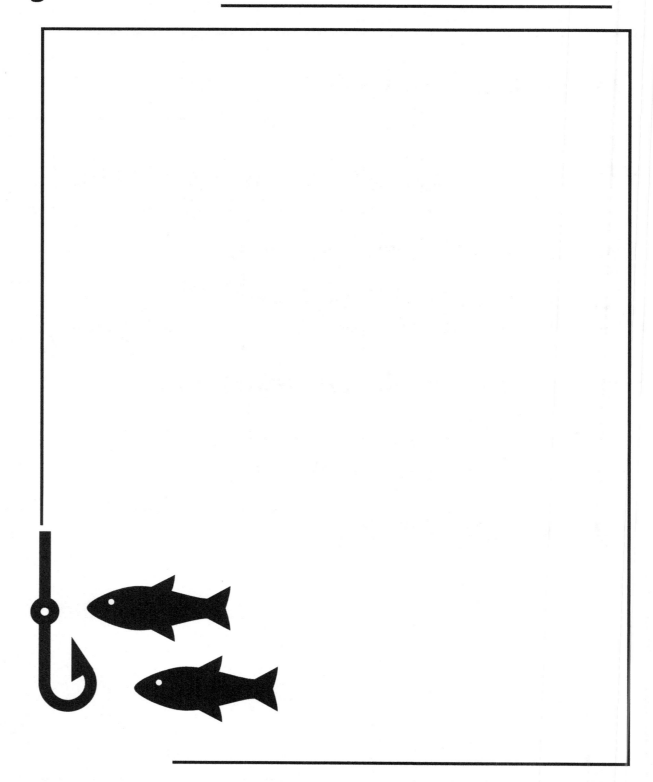

Date:
Location:
Today I Went Fishing With:

_____

The Lure I Used Was:

_____

Weather 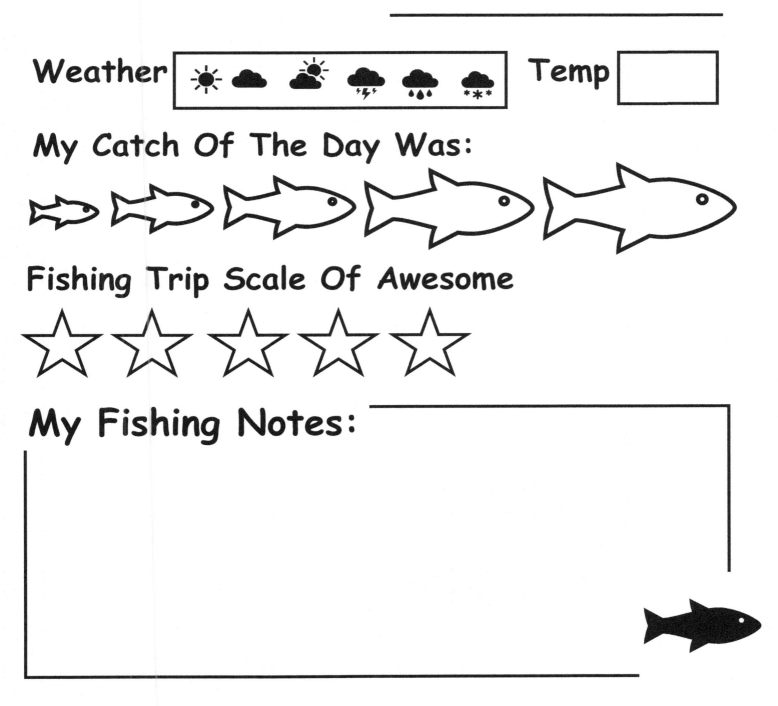 Temp

My Catch Of The Day Was:

Fishing Trip Scale Of Awesome

My Fishing Notes:

Date: _____

Fishing Discoveries: _____

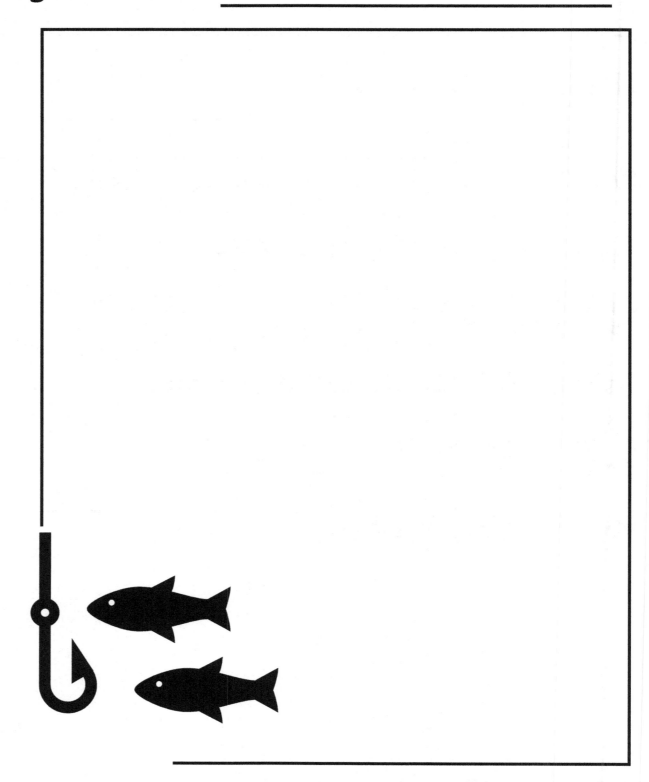

Date:

Location:

Today I Went Fishing With:

_____

The Lure I Used Was:

_____

Weather 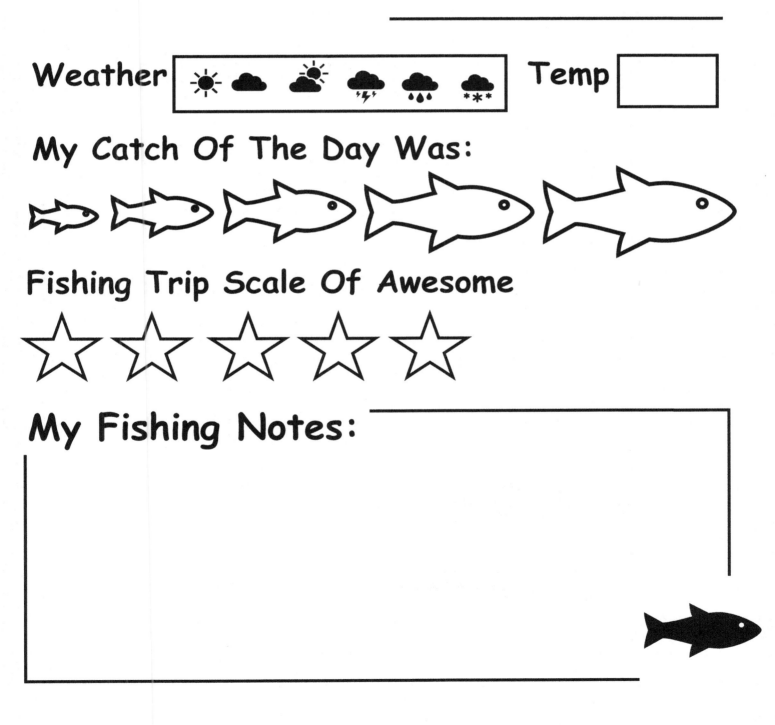 Temp

My Catch Of The Day Was:

Fishing Trip Scale Of Awesome

My Fishing Notes:

Date: _____

Fishing Discoveries: _____

Date:

Location:

Today I Went Fishing With:

_____

The Lure I Used Was:

_____

Weather 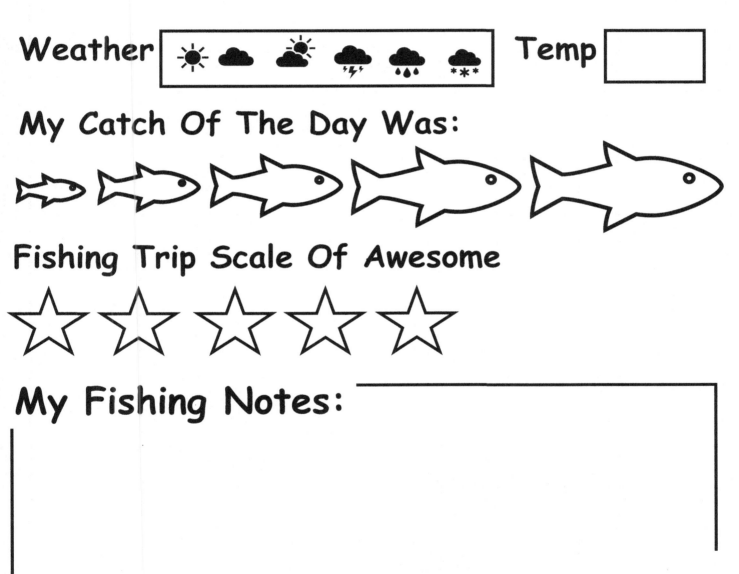   Temp ▢

My Catch Of The Day Was:

Fishing Trip Scale Of Awesome

☆ ☆ ☆ ☆ ☆

My Fishing Notes:

Date: _____

Fishing Discoveries: _____

Date:
Location:
Today I Went Fishing With:

_____

The Lure I Used Was:

_____

Weather 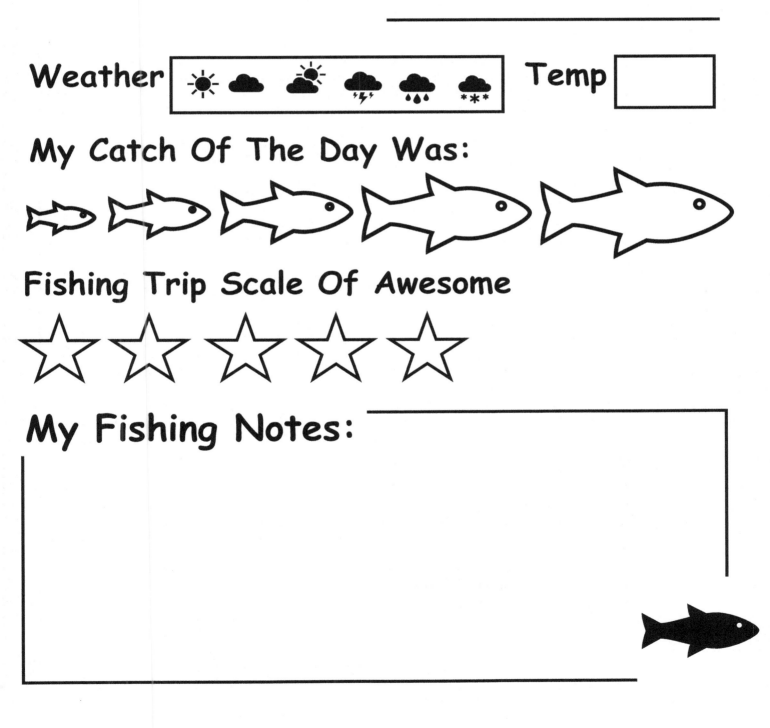 Temp

My Catch Of The Day Was:

Fishing Trip Scale Of Awesome

My Fishing Notes:

Date: _____

Fishing Discoveries: _____

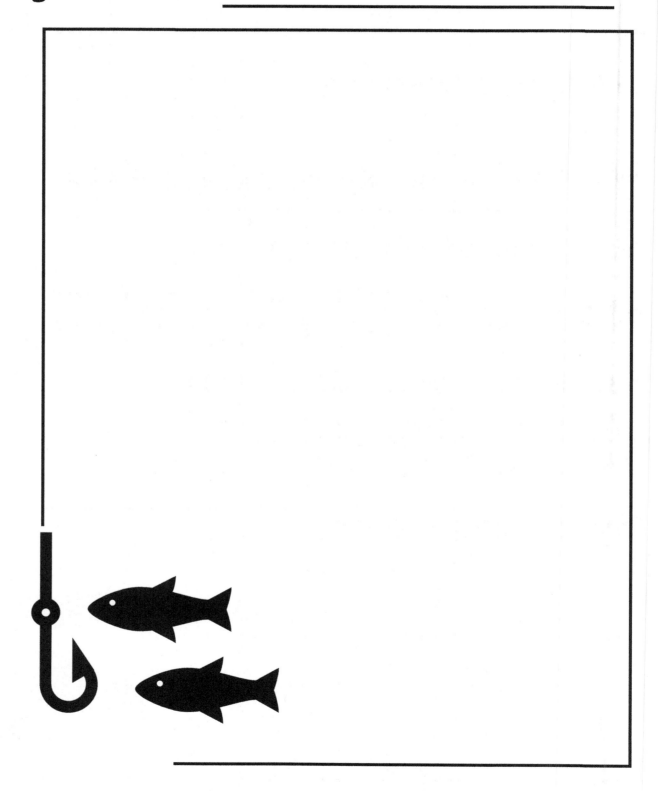

Date:
Location:
Today I Went Fishing With:

_____

The Lure I Used Was:

_____

Weather 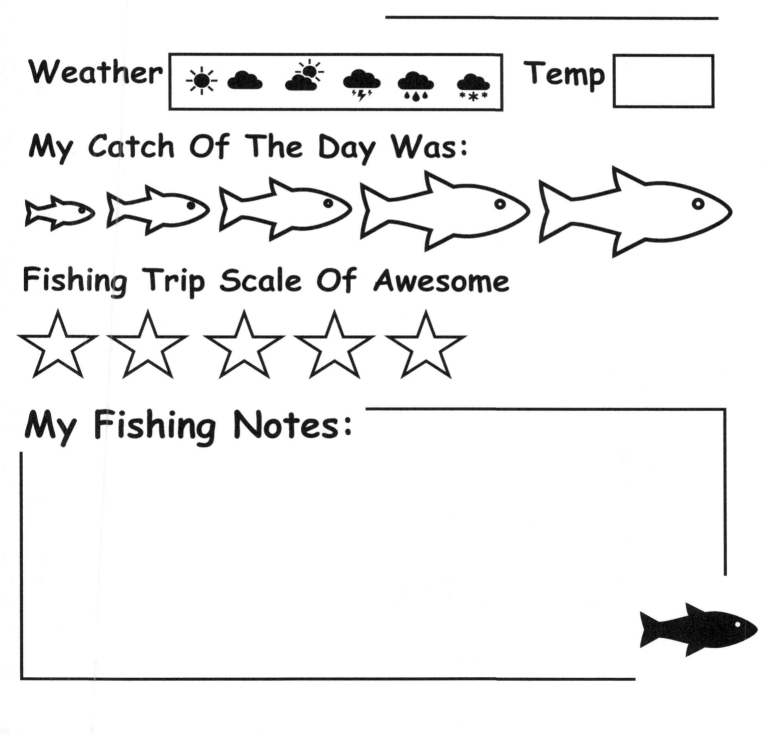 Temp

My Catch Of The Day Was:

Fishing Trip Scale Of Awesome

My Fishing Notes:

Date: _____

Fishing Discoveries:_____

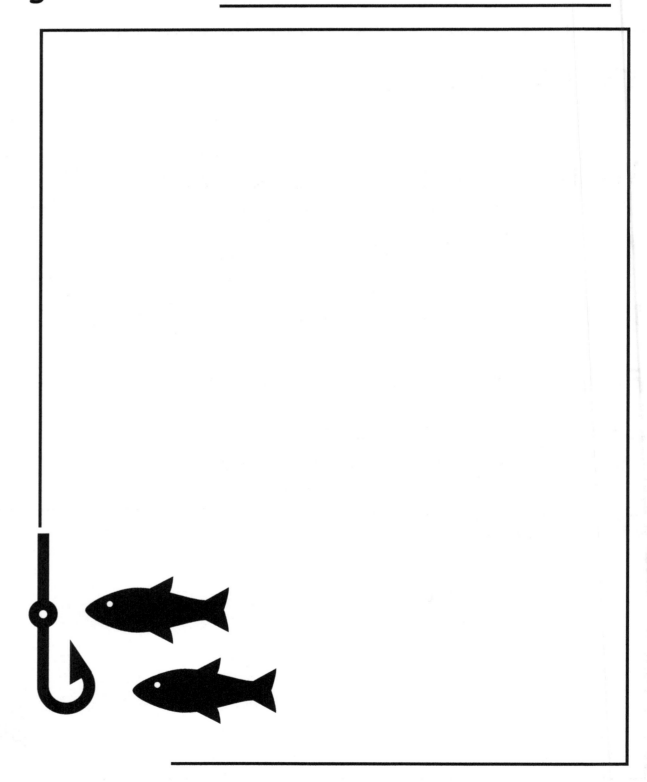

Date:
Location:
Today I Went Fishing With:

_____

The Lure I Used Was:

_____

Weather 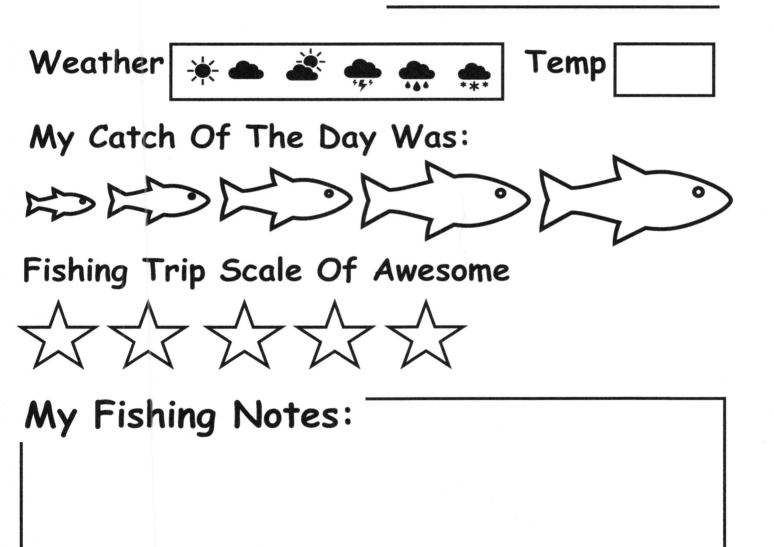 Temp

My Catch Of The Day Was:

Fishing Trip Scale Of Awesome

My Fishing Notes:

Date: _____

Fishing Discoveries: _____

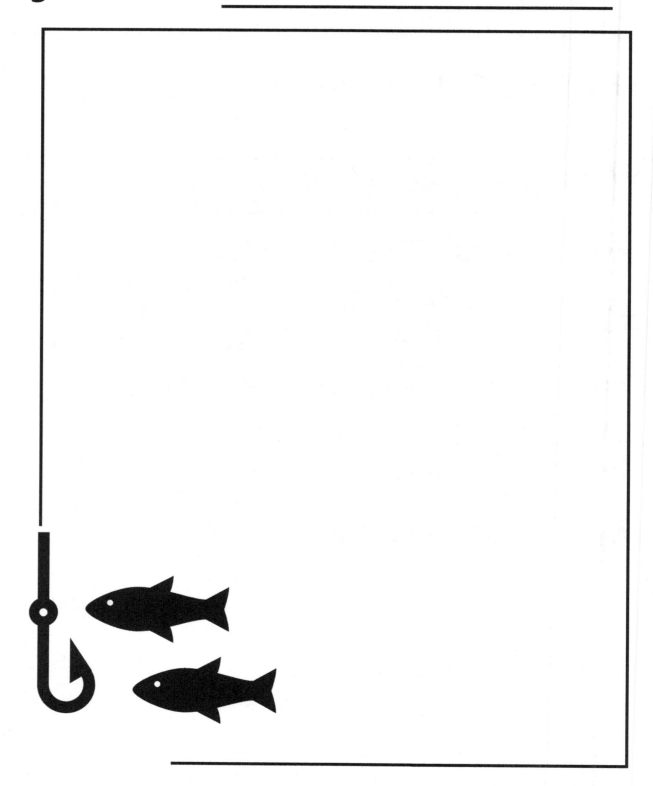

Date:

Location:

Today I Went Fishing With:

_____

The Lure I Used Was:

Weather 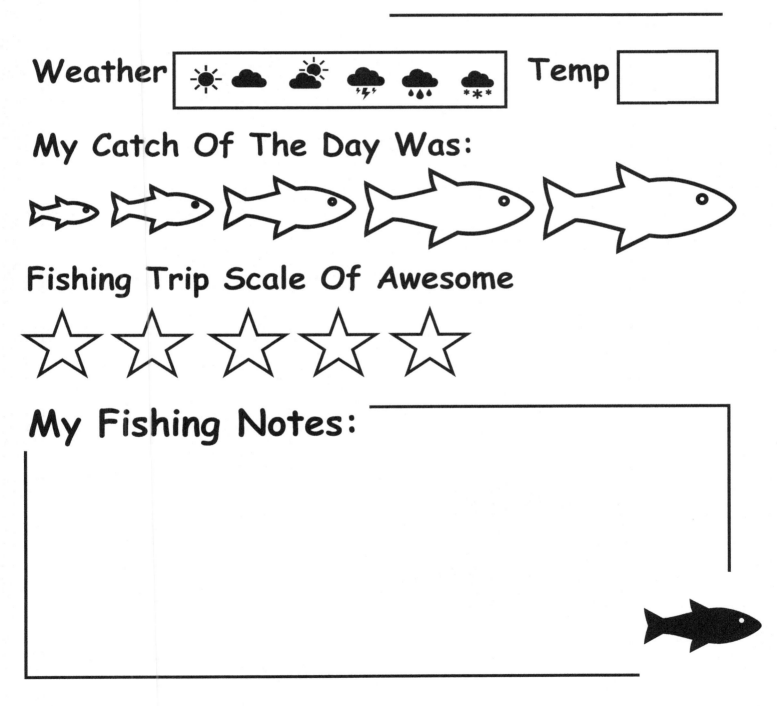 Temp

My Catch Of The Day Was:

Fishing Trip Scale Of Awesome

My Fishing Notes:

Date: _____

Fishing Discoveries: _____

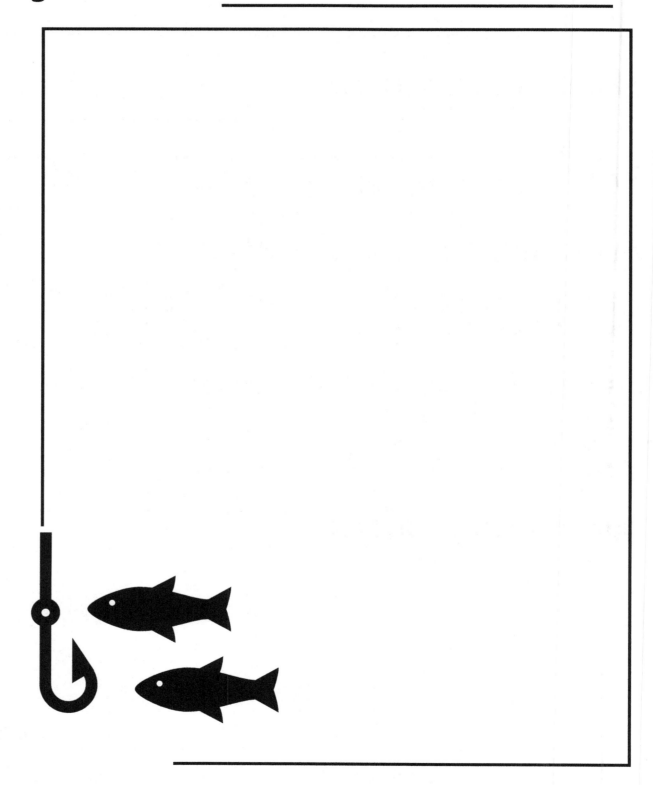

Date:

Location:

Today I Went Fishing With:

_____

The Lure I Used Was:

_____

Weather 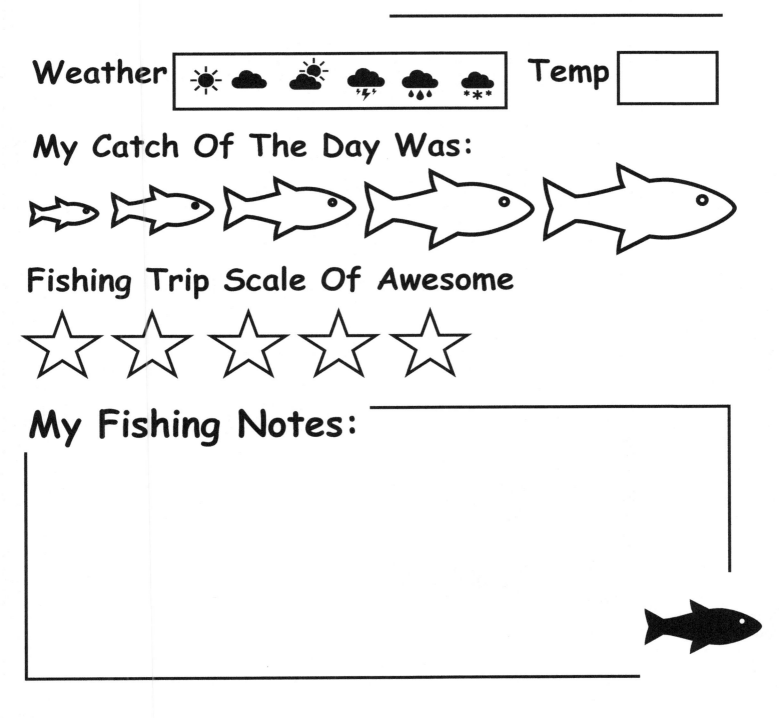 Temp

My Catch Of The Day Was:

Fishing Trip Scale Of Awesome

My Fishing Notes:

Date: _____

Fishing Discoveries: _____

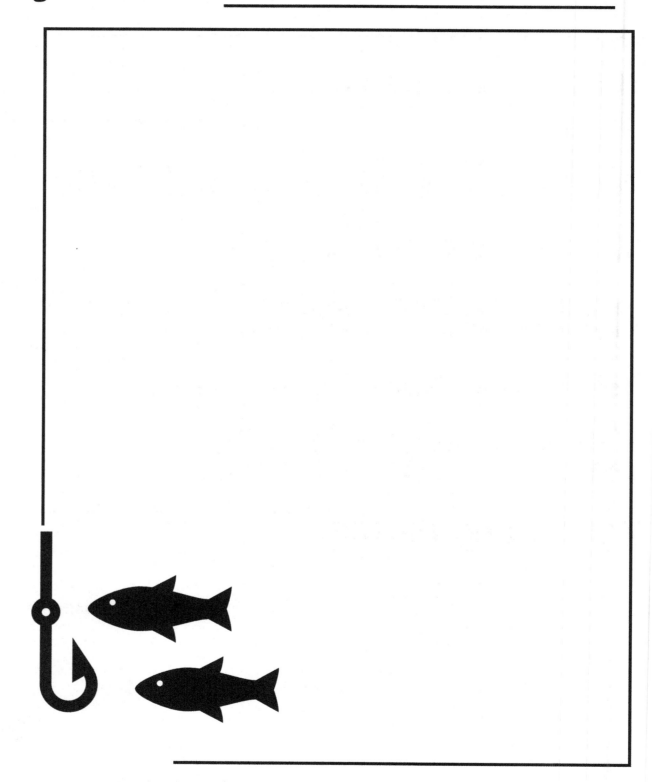

Date:
Location:
Today I Went Fishing With:

_____

The Lure I Used Was:

_____

Weather 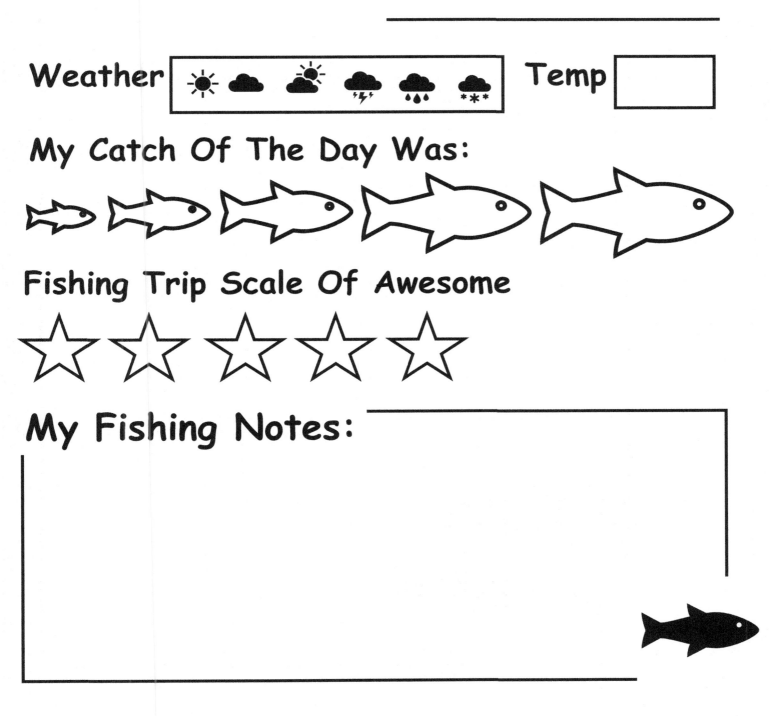 Temp

My Catch Of The Day Was:

Fishing Trip Scale Of Awesome

My Fishing Notes:

Date: _____

Fishing Discoveries: _____

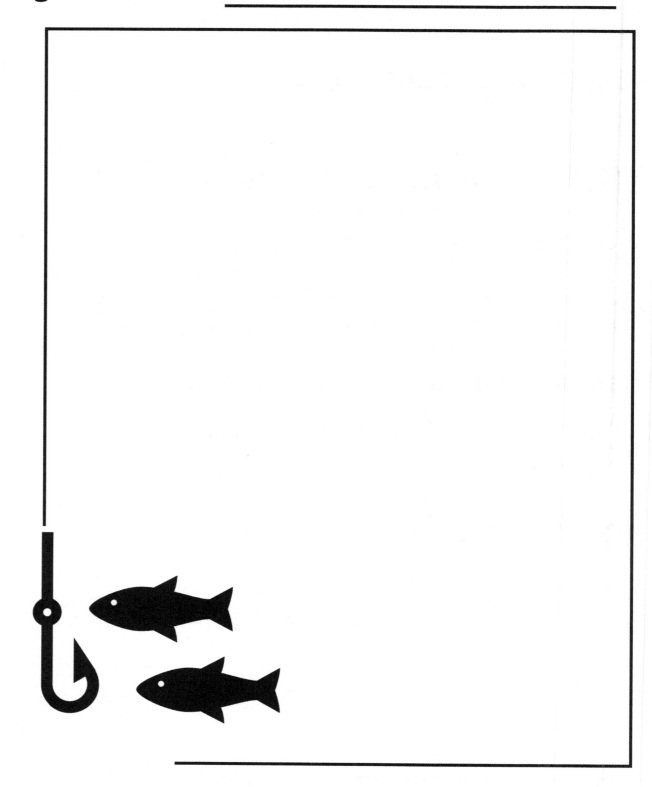

Date:
Location:
Today I Went Fishing With:

_____

The Lure I Used Was:

_____

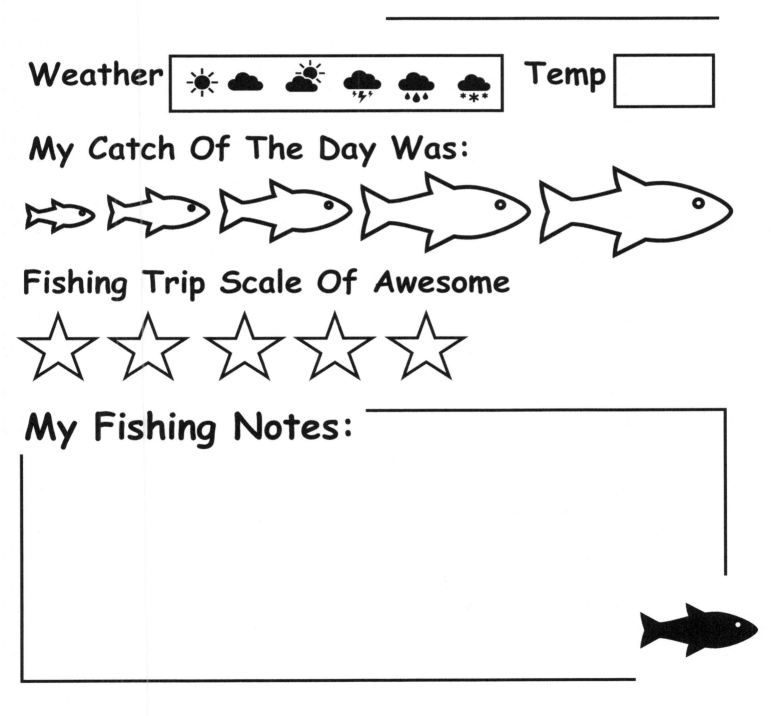

Weather

Temp

My Catch Of The Day Was:

Fishing Trip Scale Of Awesome

My Fishing Notes:

Date: _____

Fishing Discoveries: _____

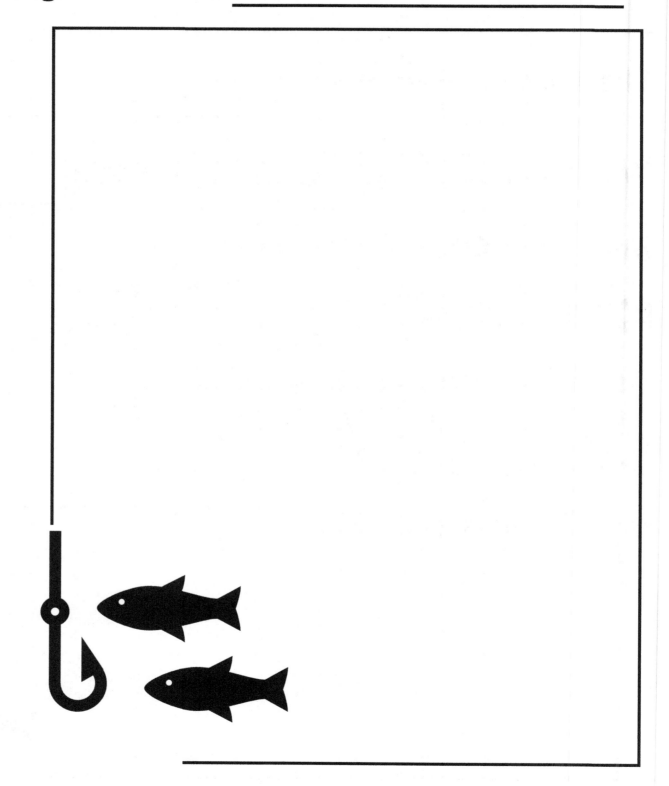

Date:
Location:
Today I Went Fishing With:

_____

The Lure I Used Was:

_____

Weather 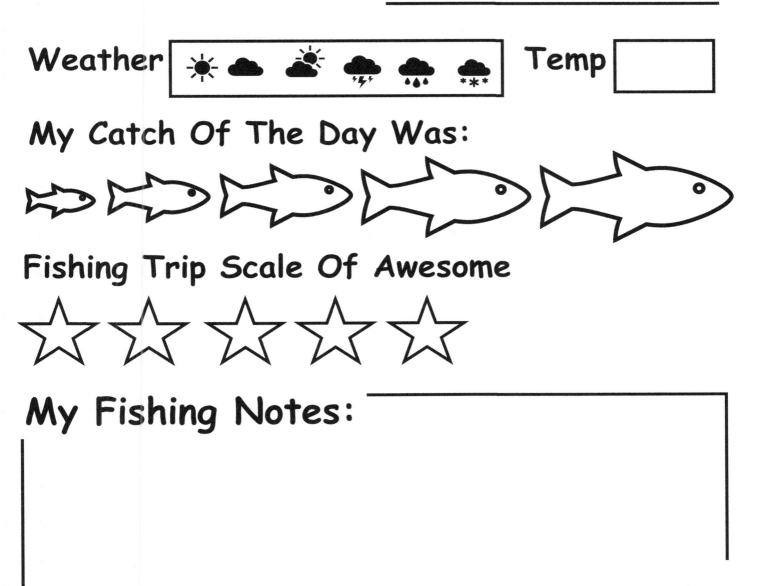 Temp

My Catch Of The Day Was:

Fishing Trip Scale Of Awesome

My Fishing Notes:

Date: _____

Fishing Discoveries: _____

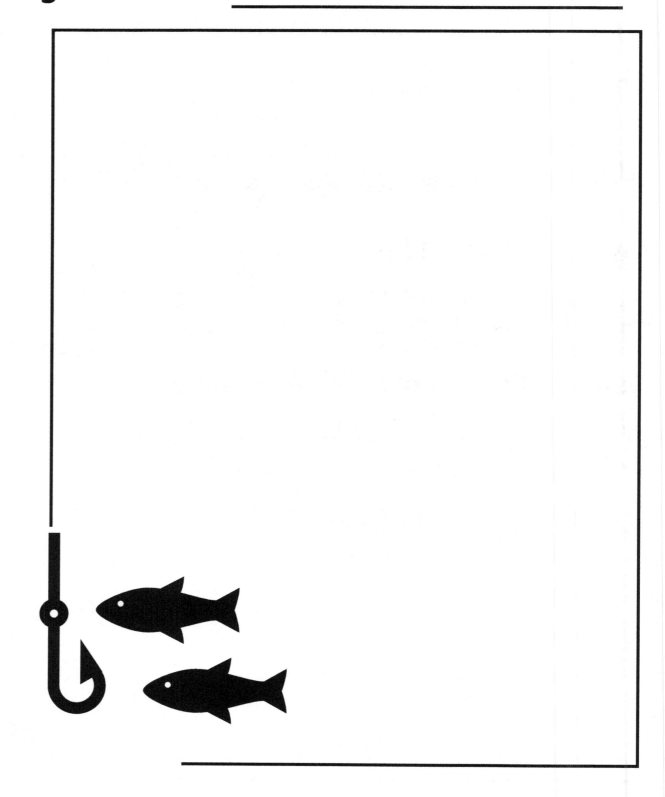

Date:
Location:
Today I Went Fishing With:

The Lure I Used Was:

Weather 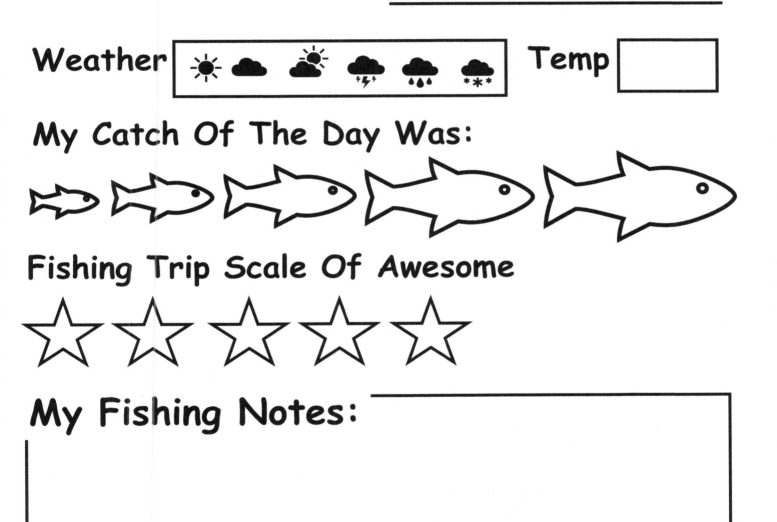 Temp

My Catch Of The Day Was:

Fishing Trip Scale Of Awesome

My Fishing Notes:

Date: _____

Fishing Discoveries: _____

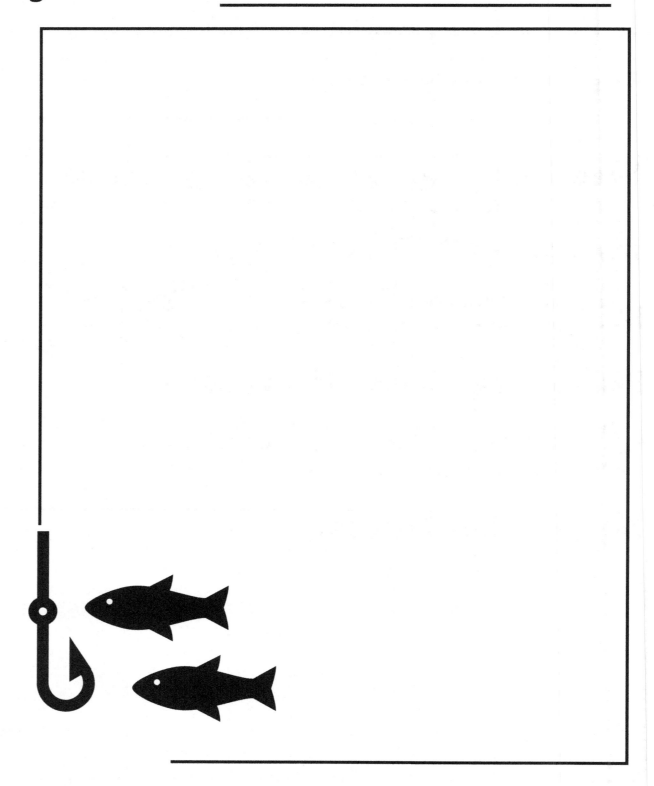

Date:
Location:
Today I Went Fishing With:

_____

The Lure I Used Was: _____

Weather 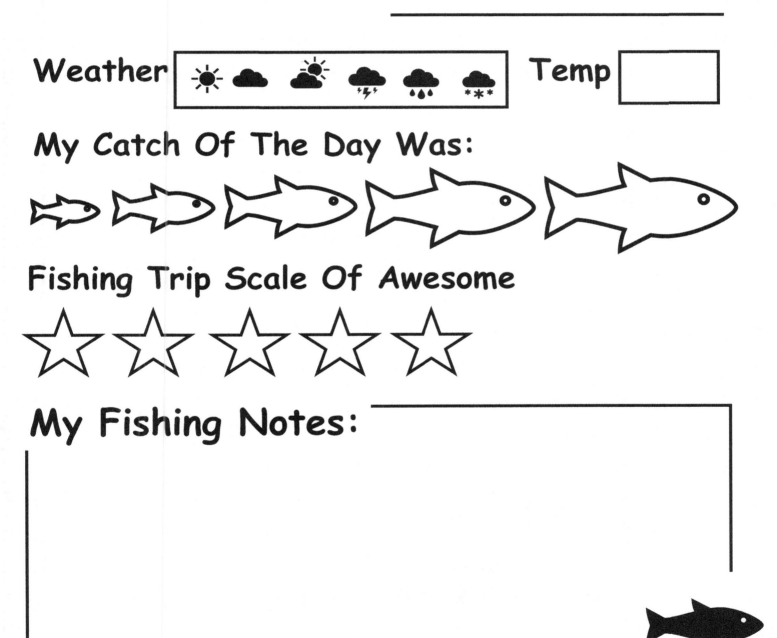 Temp

My Catch Of The Day Was:

Fishing Trip Scale Of Awesome

My Fishing Notes:

Date: _____

Fishing Discoveries: _____

Date:
Location:
Today I Went Fishing With:

_____

The Lure I Used Was:

_____

Weather 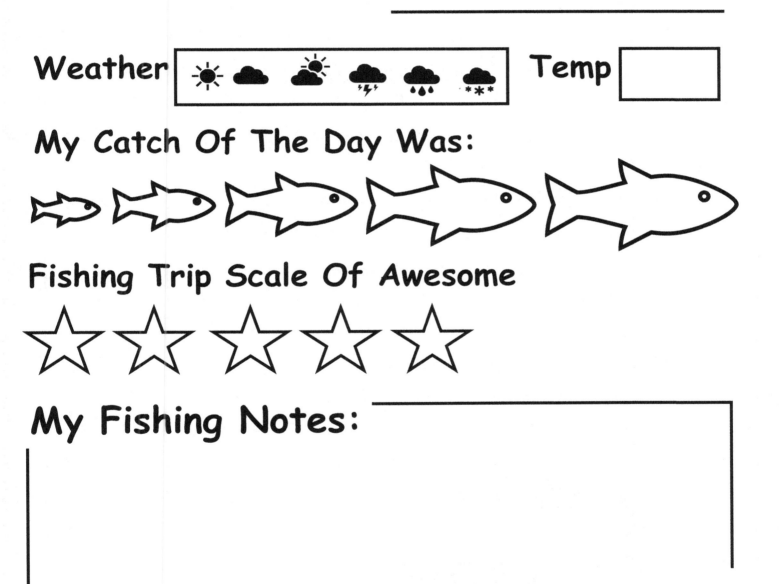 Temp

My Catch Of The Day Was:

Fishing Trip Scale Of Awesome

My Fishing Notes:

Date: _____

Fishing Discoveries: _____

Date:
Location:
Today I Went Fishing With:

_____

The Lure I Used Was:

_____

Weather 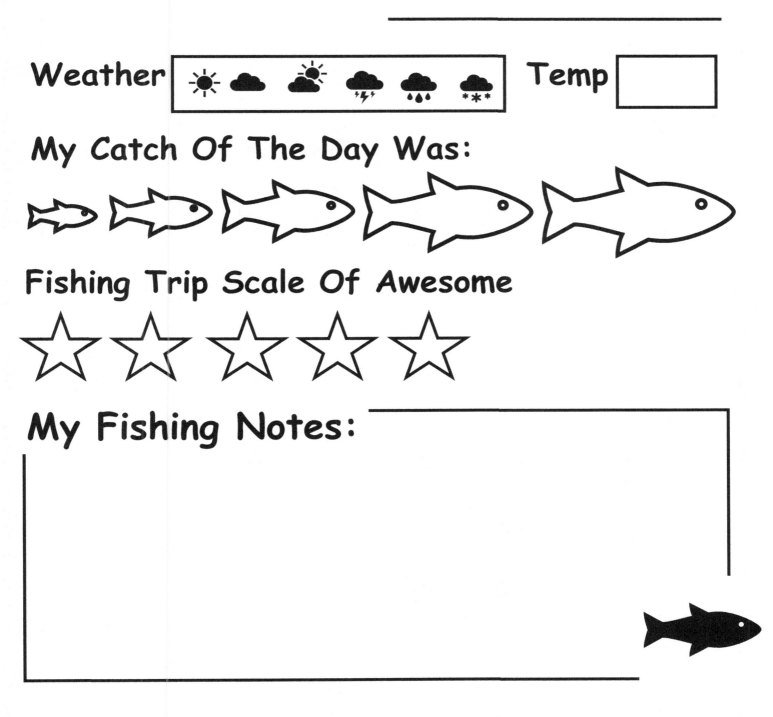 Temp

My Catch Of The Day Was:

Fishing Trip Scale Of Awesome

My Fishing Notes:

Date: _____

Fishing Discoveries: _____

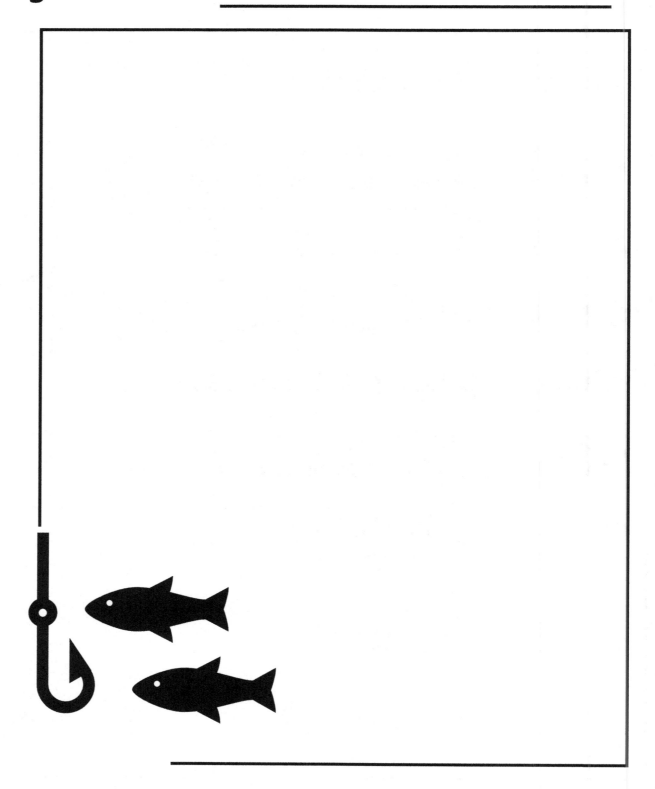

Date:
Location:
Today I Went Fishing With:
_____

The Lure I Used Was:
_____

Weather 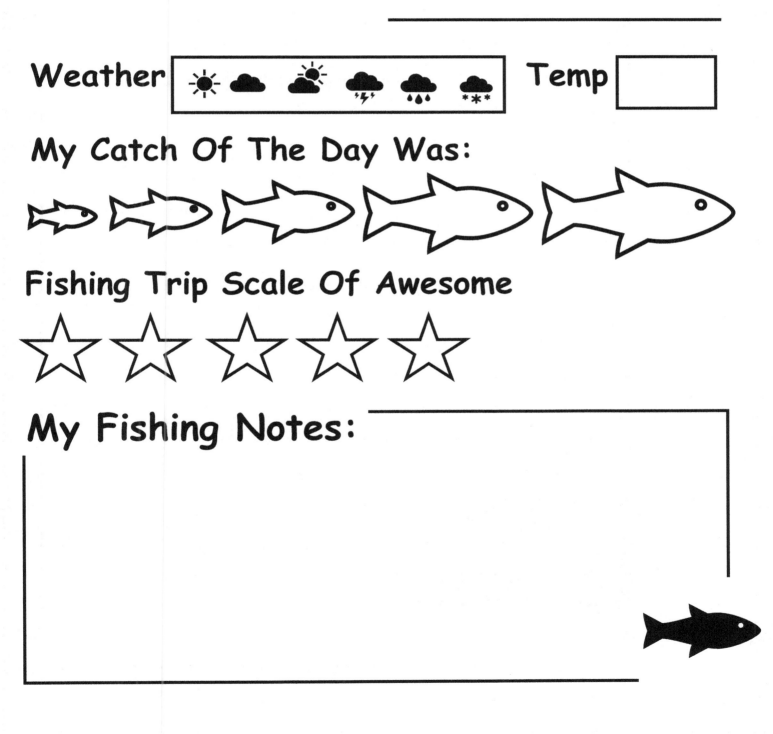 Temp ☐

My Catch Of The Day Was:

Fishing Trip Scale Of Awesome
☆ ☆ ☆ ☆ ☆

My Fishing Notes:

Date: _____

Fishing Discoveries: _____

Date:
Location:
Today I Went Fishing With:

_____

The Lure I Used Was:

_____

Weather 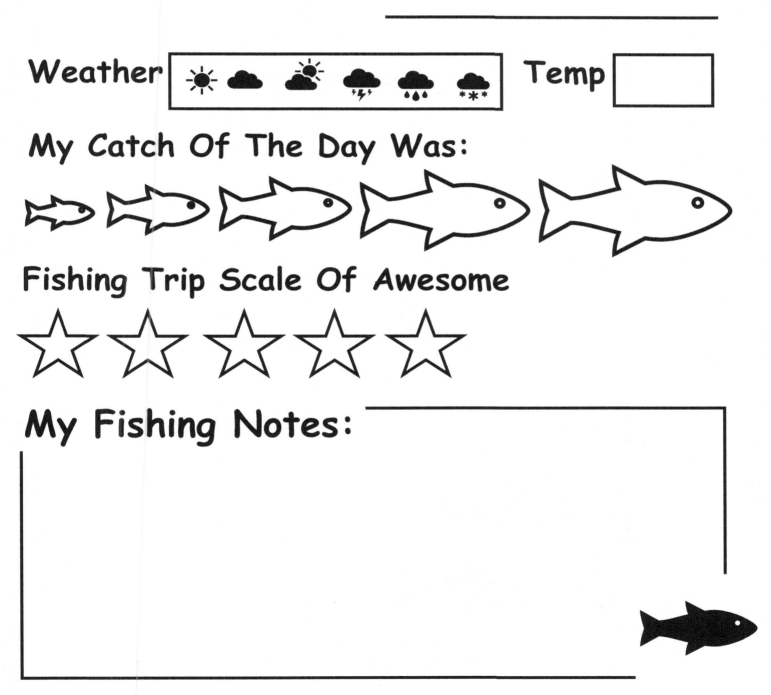 Temp

My Catch Of The Day Was:

Fishing Trip Scale Of Awesome

My Fishing Notes:

Date: _____

Fishing Discoveries:_____

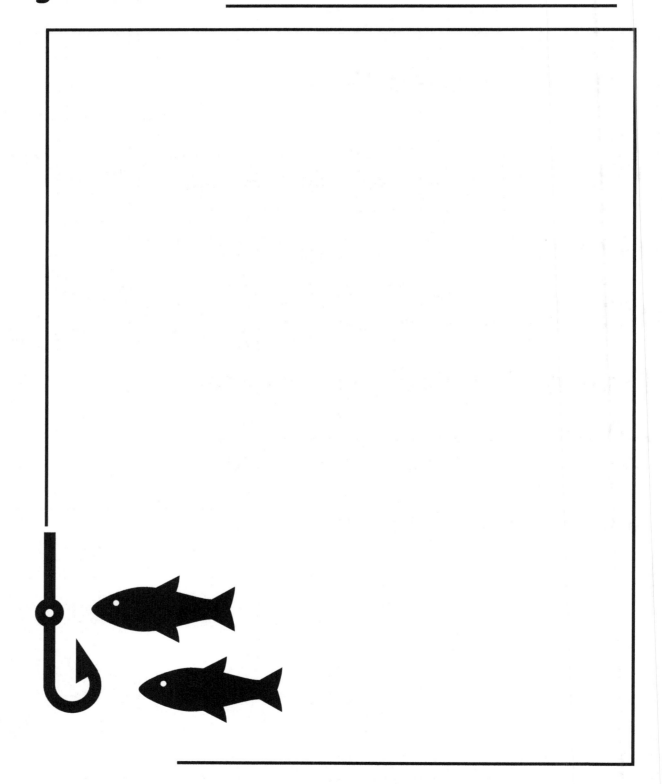

Date:

Location:

Today I Went Fishing With:

_____

The Lure I Used Was:

_____

Weather 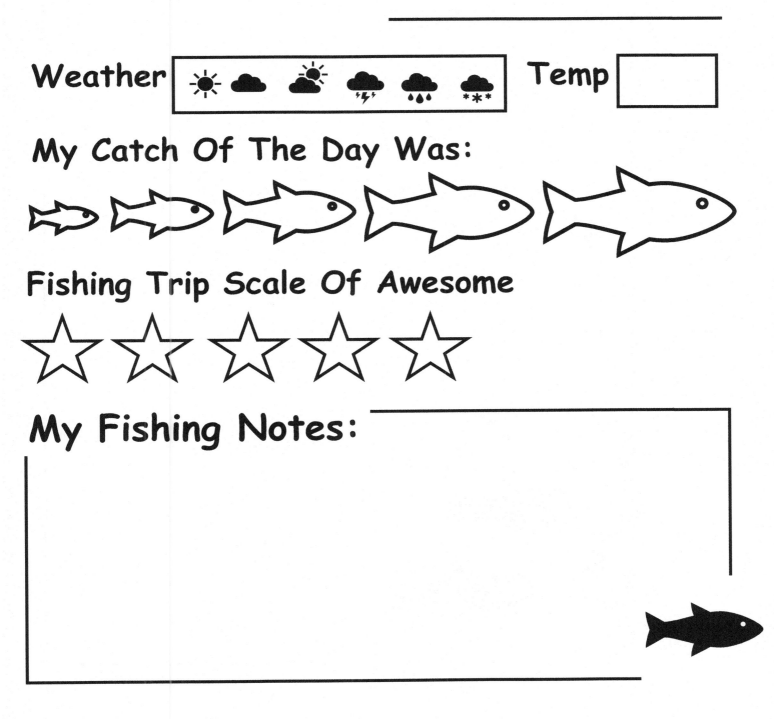 Temp

My Catch Of The Day Was:

Fishing Trip Scale Of Awesome

My Fishing Notes:

Date: _____

Fishing Discoveries: _____

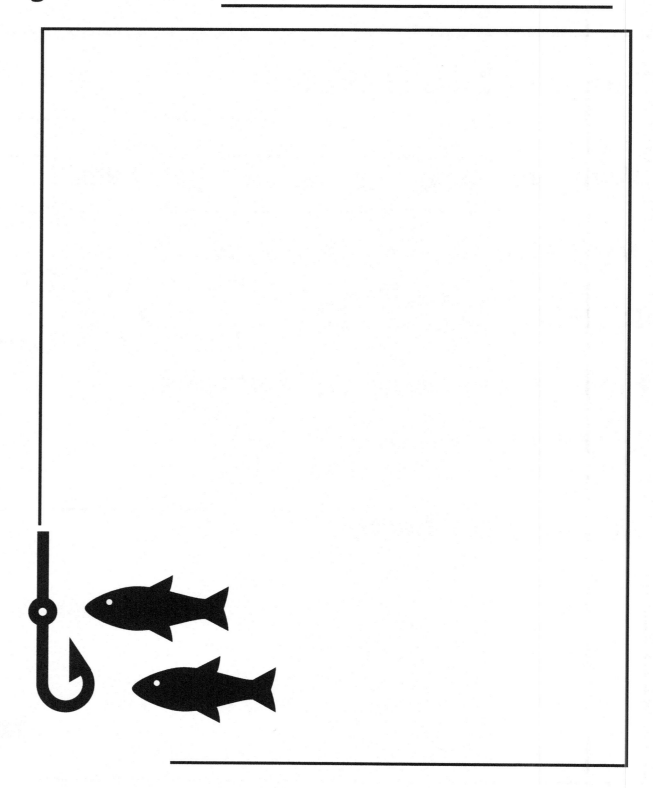

Date:

Location:

Today I Went Fishing With:

_____

The Lure I Used Was:

Weather 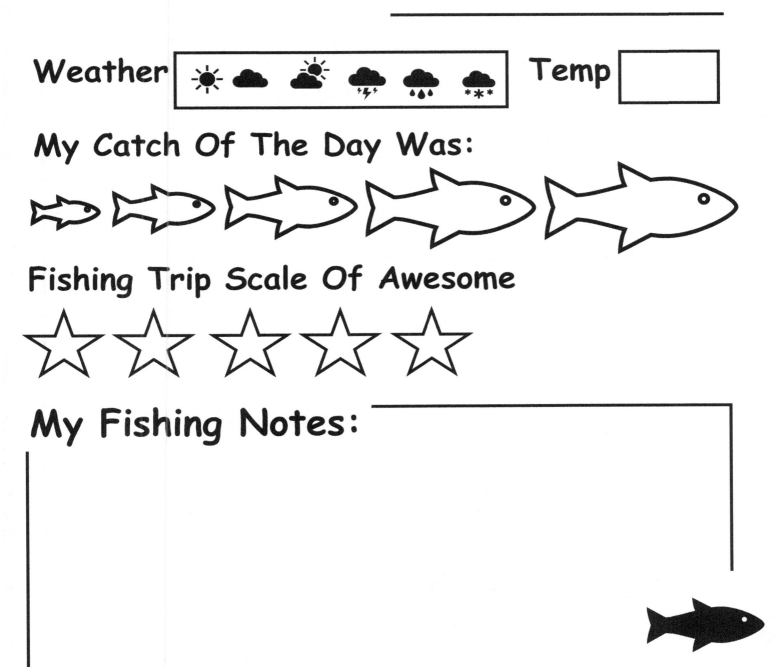 Temp

My Catch Of The Day Was:

Fishing Trip Scale Of Awesome

My Fishing Notes:

Date: _____

Fishing Discoveries: _____

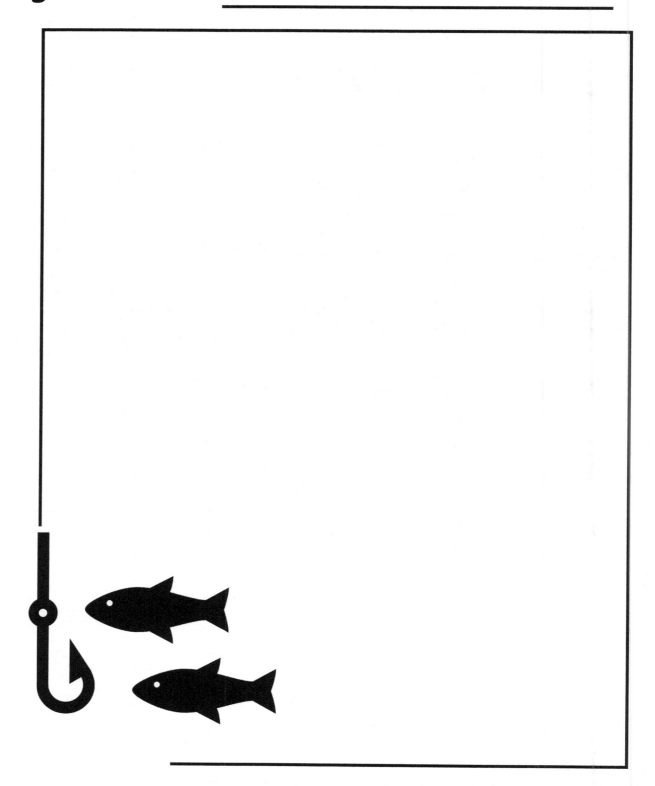

Date:

Location:

Today I Went Fishing With:

_____

The Lure I Used Was:

_____

Weather 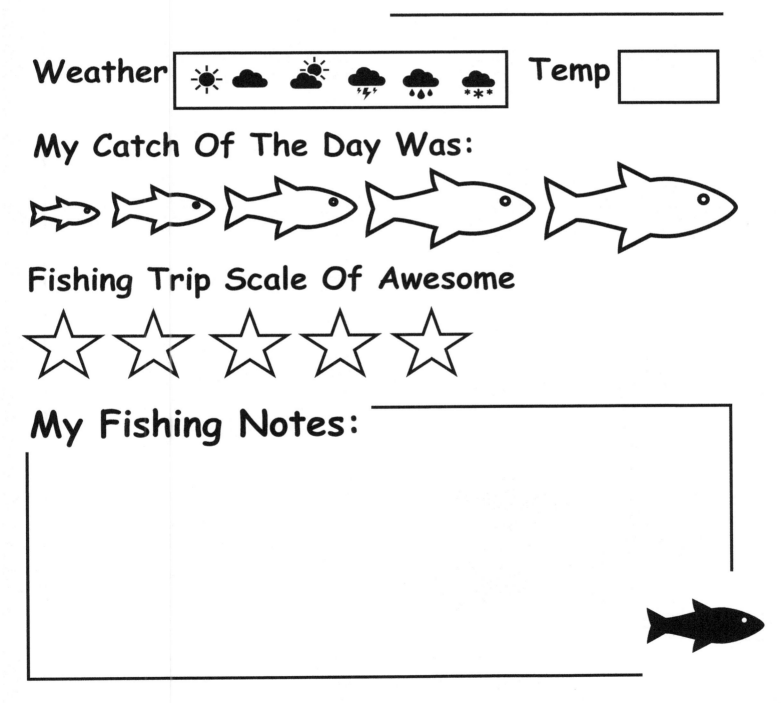 Temp

My Catch Of The Day Was:

Fishing Trip Scale Of Awesome

My Fishing Notes:

Date: _____

Fishing Discoveries: _____

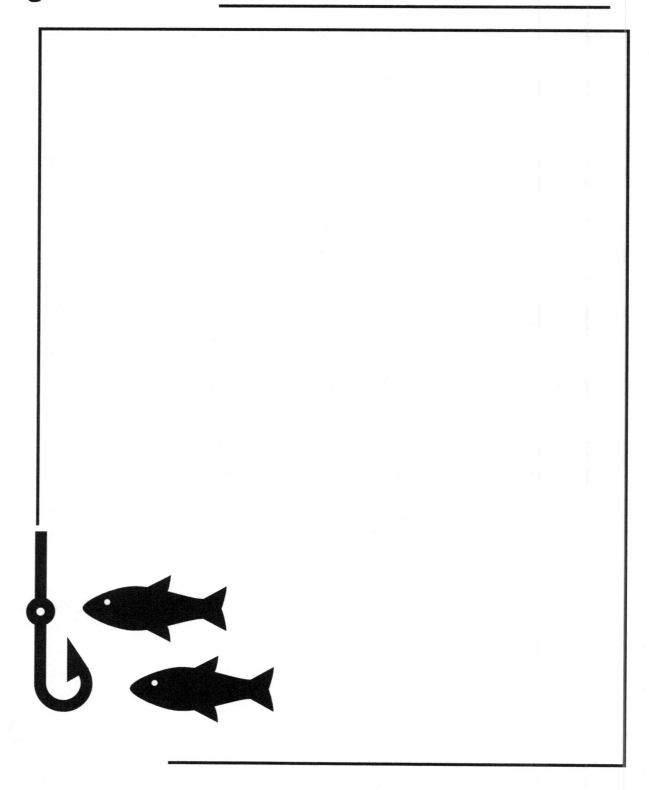

Date:
Location:
Today I Went Fishing With:

_____

The Lure I Used Was:

_____

Weather 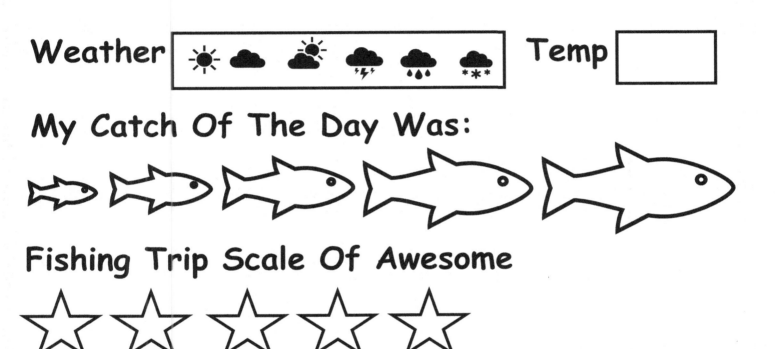 Temp [   ]

My Catch Of The Day Was:

Fishing Trip Scale Of Awesome

☆ ☆ ☆ ☆ ☆

My Fishing Notes:

Date: _____

Fishing Discoveries: _____

Date:
Location:
Today I Went Fishing With:

_____

The Lure I Used Was:

_____

Weather 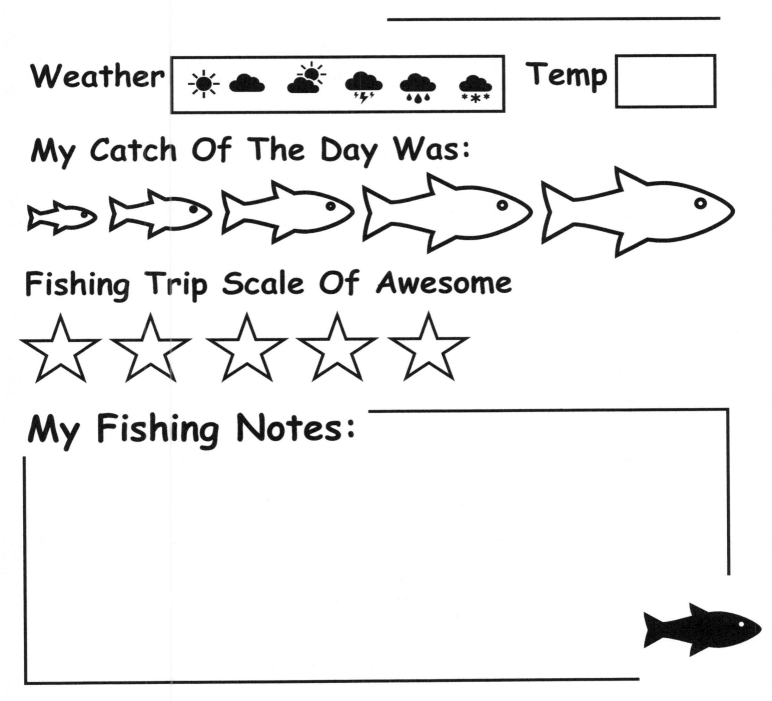 Temp

My Catch Of The Day Was:

Fishing Trip Scale Of Awesome

My Fishing Notes:

Date: _____

Fishing Discoveries: _____

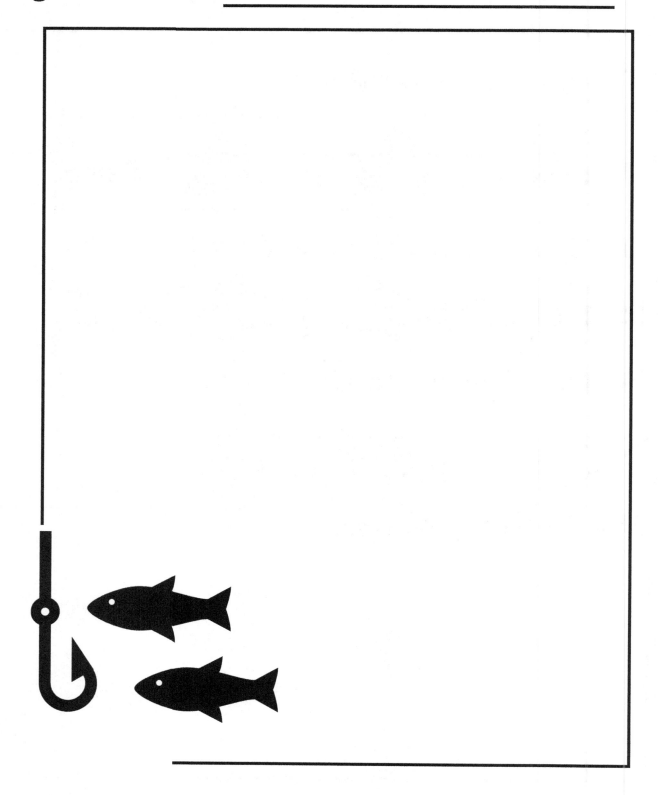

Date:
Location:
Today I Went Fishing With:

_____

The Lure I Used Was:

_____

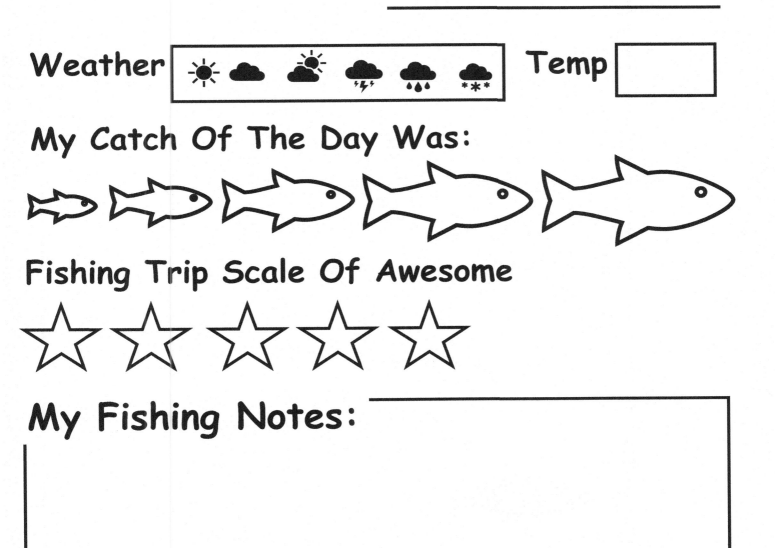

Weather

Temp

My Catch Of The Day Was:

Fishing Trip Scale Of Awesome

My Fishing Notes:

Date: _____

Fishing Discoveries: _____

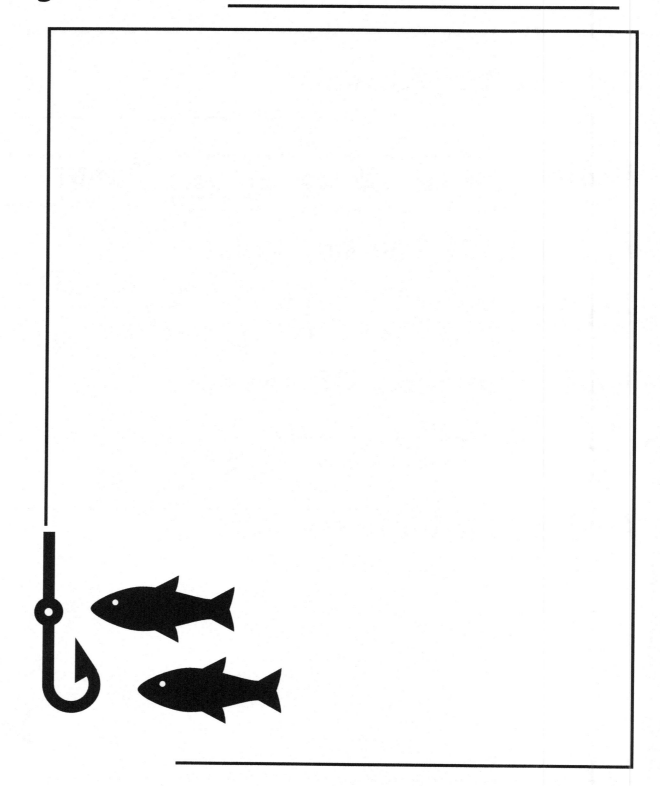

Date:
Location:
Today I Went Fishing With:

_____

The Lure I Used Was:

_____

Weather 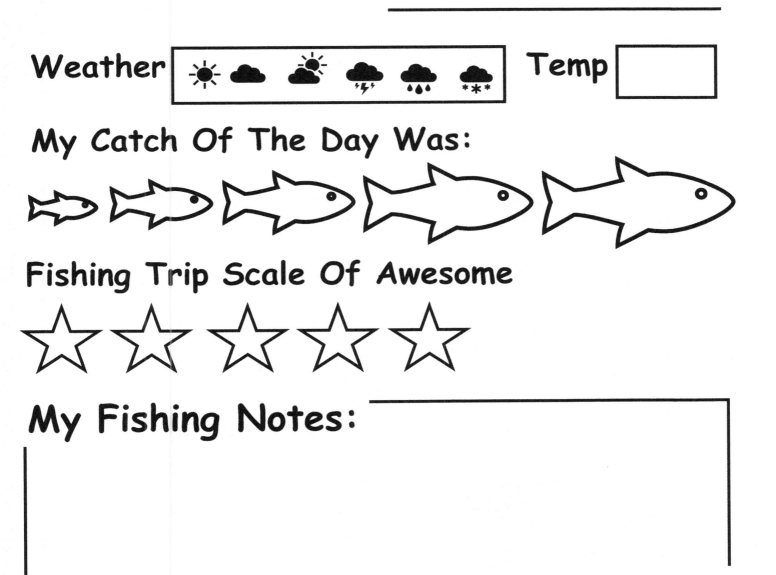 Temp

My Catch Of The Day Was:

Fishing Trip Scale Of Awesome

My Fishing Notes:

Date: _____

Fishing Discoveries: _____

Date:
Location:
Today I Went Fishing With:

_____

The Lure I Used Was:

_____

Weather 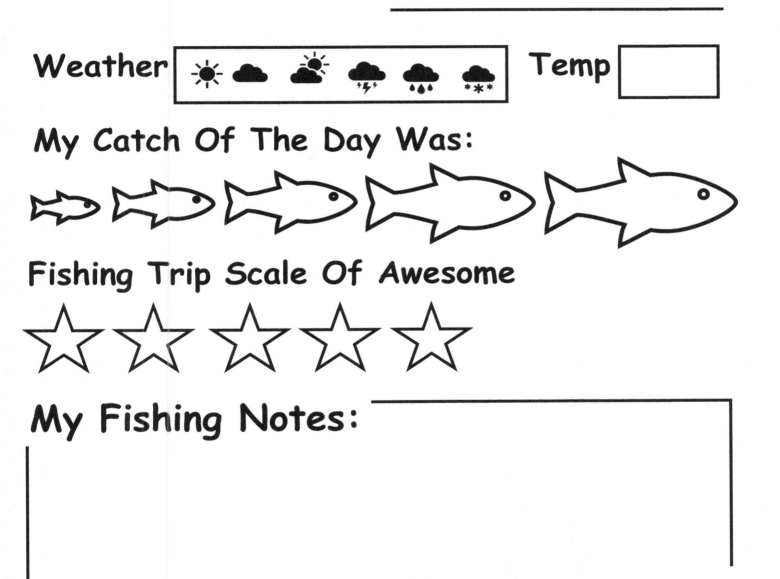 Temp

My Catch Of The Day Was:

Fishing Trip Scale Of Awesome

My Fishing Notes:

Date: _____

Fishing Discoveries: _____

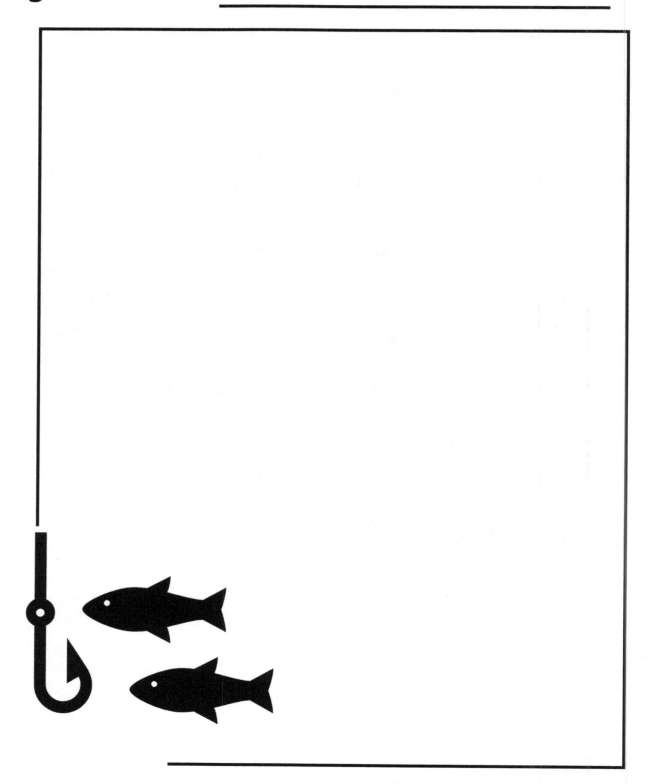

Date:
Location:
Today I Went Fishing With:

_____

The Lure I Used Was:

_____

Weather 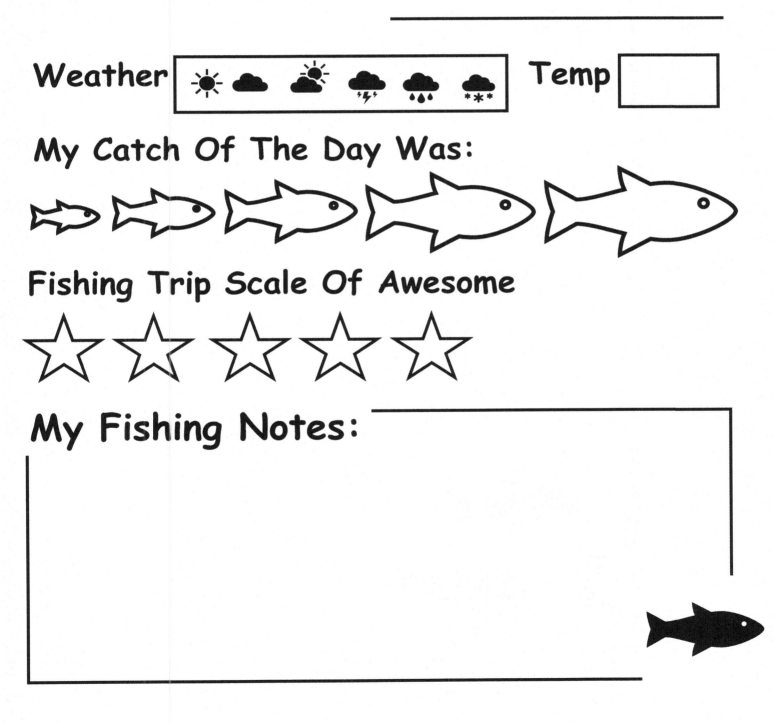 Temp

My Catch Of The Day Was:

Fishing Trip Scale Of Awesome

My Fishing Notes:

Date: _____

Fishing Discoveries: _____

Date:

Location:

Today I Went Fishing With:

_____

The Lure I Used Was:

_____

Weather 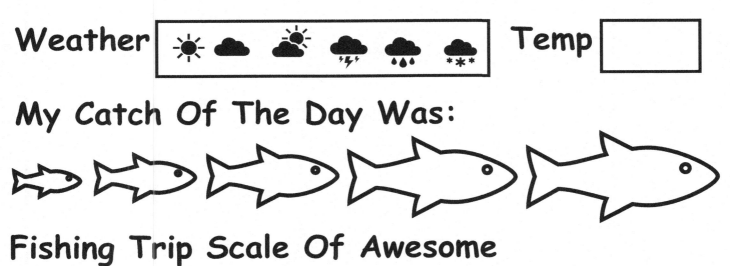 Temp

My Catch Of The Day Was:

Fishing Trip Scale Of Awesome

☆ ☆ ☆ ☆ ☆

My Fishing Notes:

Date: _____

Fishing Discoveries: _____

Made in the USA
Columbia, SC
26 April 2020